0 7 NOV 2013

NC

BC

100 alternative career options

You want to do what?!

100 alternative career options

Kathleen Houston

3rd edition

You want to do what?!

This third edition published in 2009 by Trotman Publishing, a division of Crimson Publishing Ltd, Westminster House, Kew Road, Richmond, Surrey TW9 2ND

© Trotman Publishing 2009

First edition published in 2001
Second edition, published in two volumes, in 2003 by Trotman and Co Ltd

Author Kathleen Houston

British Library Cataloguing in Publication Data
A catalogue record for this book is available from the British Library

ISBN 978 1 84455 176 7

Typeset by Cambridge Publishing Management Ltd
Printed and bound in Great Britain by Athenaeum Press, Gateshead

Contents

M

N

O

P

R

S

About the Author

Kathleen Houston is a working Careers Adviser, professional Career Coach, University Lecturer and Motivational Trainer. She has experience of advising university, college and school students, as well as mature career-returners. She is a regular contributor to national and local radio stations, most recently contributing to BBC Radio 1, Radio 2 and Radio 5 Live programmes on career-related topics. She is enthusiastic about helping people pursue their dream careers and has been successful in doing just that. She believes that many people never consider the full range of options open to them. This book is designed to inspire people to consider unusual, seemingly unattainable or simply less well-known jobs.

Introduction

You probably don't want to read this because you want to skip or browse through the jobs hoping to land on something which appeals to you. That's fine, if you're not easily confused or befuddled. If you are, though, then you might wonder how the careers included were selected, and why some are featured and others not. I hope that you are curious enough about this to read on.

Well, in simple terms, to make the cut the featured careers had to satisfy certain criteria, marking them out as:

- unusual
- less well known
- misunderstood (as witnessed by the fact that people may regularly get the wrong idea about these jobs)
- popular (probably jobs that many people aspire to)
- dreamy (as in 'does anyone ever get to do that job?') or
- slightly wacky (define that any way you want but there is a shade of difference between wacky and unusual, in my mind at least).

The jobs listed are a very personal selection and are based primarily on what I thought fitted the categories above; in particular I chose jobs or careers that I found interesting or surprising in some way. I trust that within the selection there are some that will surprise and/or interest you too. Some of them are quite normal, even usual rather than unusual, and these may be showcased because I, in my opinionated way, think they deserve to be promoted because they are more interesting than they seem. On the other hand some are downright peculiar.

A Life Less Ordinary

As a Careers Adviser I often meet people who are looking for something a little less ordinary and so I have aimed to offer these types of jobs for your consideration. You will find a broad range of career ideas, including those requiring high-level qualifications as well as those which may take less training time and can be accessed with lower-level qualifications. It does seem to me that the more appealing careers often require the most challenging qualifications or lengthy training, but it is up to you to decide whether something is worth the necessary effort.

The Way The Book Is Organised

This book is designed for those of us (me included) with the attention span of a goldfish, so it is organised into neat sections with regular headings to signpost you and keep you interested. I want you to learn just enough to trigger you into finding out more, and the 'Contacts' section at the end of each featured career will take you further.

Qualifications

If no qualifications are specified (this is rare) it is because something else, such as talent or personality, is the essential requirement. Otherwise clear qualification guidelines are offered.

Qualifications are changing all the time and new ones frequently emerge. Just when you think you have got the hang of these, government education experts start talking about Level 2 or Level 3 qualifications and confusion returns. So below you will find an attempt to make things clearer.

Understanding The Code

Certain words or phrases are used regularly in each career section and below is a guide to what this kind of shorthand, or code, means.

Level 1, 2 or 3 etc. – Many jobs will require a minimum level – for example, a Level 2 or Level 3 qualification – so take a note of the details opposite and bear in mind the level you are studying at, whatever your eventual qualification.

Good GCSE Profile – This is normally required by employers and universities and, as a rule, means 4–5 GCSE pass grades at C grade and above, including English and maths. This might include the Higher Diploma taken from Year 10 in schools.

Or Equivalent – A catch-all phrase to cover other equivalent qualifications that might exist, including standard Scottish qualifications, international variations and other less common qualifications which you may come across or even already possess.

A Levels/Diploma Level Or Equivalent – This means a Level 3 qualification of some kind. The diploma in this case would be the Progression or Advanced Diploma.

Starting Salary – This is generally an idea of the salary that you might start your career on. Higher salary grades will be dependent on where you live and work and how you progress through your career.

Competition Is Intense – For many reasons certain careers are extremely popular and success in gaining a place on a course or a first job may be a great deal to do with a combination of luck, talent, determination and using your personal contacts. It is important that you know what you are up against, but do not allow yourself to be put off your dream career. This is meant as an essential reality check that will hopefully make you better informed about what it will take, and aware of what you can do, to be successful.

QUALIFICATIONS

- National Vocational Qualifications (NVQs) – in-work setting where you learn as you do the job
  Levels 1, 2 and 3 (but higher levels also available)

Foundation qualifications
- Foundation Diploma
  Foundation course

- NVQ course
  BTEC Introductory course

Intermediate qualifications
- Higher Diploma
- Intermediate/BTEC First/VRQ (Vocationally Related Qualifications)

Advanced qualifications
- Advanced level/A levels in applied subjects
- BTEC National Diploma
- Progression/Advanced Diploma

Degree-level qualifications
- Foundation degree (2–3 years)

- Honours degree (3 years)

DETAILS

- Generally available as part of apprenticeship training – you would probably be working four days a week and attending a training centre or college one day a week – this is known as work-based training. NVQs are available for jobs such as catering, engineering, plumbing, business administration, hairdressing, leisure and many more.
  You achieve the NVQ once you can prove that you are competent in particular areas of the job role. There are no exams but you would be assessed on the job and through a portfolio which you will complete.

Normally Level 1
- You could start this from Year 10 at school (alongside GCSE subjects) and you would be able to study specialist job-related skills in subjects such as construction or IT or creative and media or society, health and development or engineering alongside basic GCSE subjects. It could take you on to college-based courses or possibly into apprenticeships. The Foundation Diploma is equivalent to five GCSE grades D–G.
- Foundation courses, NVQs and BTEC Introductory courses are one-year college-based courses which build confidence and skills and may lead on to Intermediate courses – ideal for you if you want a college experience but may not gain above an E grade at GCSE. Offered in subjects such as IT, catering, hairdressing and sport.

Normally Level 2
- Similar to the Foundation Diploma above but equivalent to seven GCSEs at grade C or over.
- If you have at least four D grades at GCSE, these one-year courses are still job/career specific and can lead into apprenticeships or to further advanced courses.

Normally Level 3
- Various advanced-level courses are available for study over two years – some in standard subjects like History and English, others in applied subjects such as accounting, business or textiles.
- BTEC National Diplomas in many subjects, including graphics, public services, engineering, children's care.
- Progression and Advanced Diplomas offer study in subjects such as construction, engineering, creative and media and IT. The Progression Diploma is equivalent to two-and-a-half A levels and the Advanced Diploma is equivalent to four-and-a-half A levels.

Most advanced-level qualifications lead into A level trainee jobs, Advanced Apprenticeships or university courses.

Normally Level 4/5/6
- Similar to HND/C (Higher National Diplomas/Certificates) – these are a new way for students to study at university, perhaps for a shorter time, and work in a job as well. Many employers are now offering jobs for A level/Advanced/Progression Diploma/BTEC students with the chance to gain a degree as well.
- Traditional degree study – often an essential requirement for certain careers.

What I Would Recommend Finally – A Plan Of Approach

Check the A to Z list of contents so you know what is included in the 100 career list.

Flick through the book and pause when something catches your eye.

Read, consider and score a career out of 10 (with 10 out of 10 meaning a high match) according to how well suited you think you are to that particular job, based on:

- personality match
- skills match
- 'your potential to do the job well'
- motivation interest/match (how excited you are by that career).

Those careers that return a high score are worth exploring further and then it's over to you.

So that's it – start now and find out what you want to do career wise and then take some positive action to make it a reality. One in five people are apparently unhappy in their work – make sure you find the way to be happy in your career and beat those odds. You can now take the first step by reading on – I hope you are surprised at what is possible for you.

Kath Houston

Abseiling Window Cleaner/ Rope Access Worker

If you've ever seen someone abseiling down a building cleaning windows or inspecting a suspension bridge for faults or carrying out welding work on a tall structure, then you've seen industrial rope access workers at their work. Window cleaning previously meant ugly scaffolding or expensive cradles to support the cleaners as they worked – rope access workers provide a speedy, high-quality alternative to old-fashioned window cleaning. Rope access workers can also be seen in a range of cleaning/painting/maintenance roles for civil engineering companies or local councils, or just putting up advertising hoardings on unsightly buildings which are under repair, in order to improve the city skyline. They might also be used for oil and gas platform maintenance, on construction sites, for telecommunications masts or for the police, fire and rescue services.

The Job Description
Rope access workers find the best way to establish a safe working position at height or in areas of difficult access. They use abseiling and caving techniques to position themselves to undertake work including the inspection, testing and surveying of large structures (such as bridges, chimneys or skyscrapers), or cleaning and painting work, including spray painting and grit blasting. As a general rule rope access workers are attached to two separate ropes and each rope has a separate anchorage point so that there is always a safety rope in case the working rope becomes damaged. Safety is paramount in this work and workers do their work in pairs using rope attachments and equipment, which are attached to their harnesses. Often rope access workers have a qualification in welding or painting and decorating or surveying as well as rope access qualifications.

The Person Specification
Although this work sounds as if it might be suited to people who are addicted to danger and risk, it is far more likely that it will suit you if you want an outdoor/active job with the excitement of abseiling and the ability to work at great heights in a safe and high-quality way. For this work you would need to be:

- experienced and interested in abseiling and outdoor pursuits (from having done this as a hobby – it is not absolutely necessary to have abseiling/caving qualifications, as specialist rope access training is normally compulsory for this work for insurance purposes)
- able to work at heights

- good with your hands and willing to do a physically demanding job
- committed to health and safety procedures.

What It Takes

Most people who go into this work have previously enjoyed abseiling, climbing or caving as a hobby and have considerable skill and experience already. Some are ex-forces personnel who have learned these skills through army training, for example. It would help if you had taken National Governing Board qualifications in abseiling and climbing – these are offered at outdoor pursuit centres and through organisations like the Outward Bound and the YMCA.

However, industry-standard qualifications have been developed which are now considered compulsory for this kind of work. These qualifications are normally approved by the Work at Height Safety Association (WAHSA), the Health and Safety Executive (HSE) and the Industrial Rope Access Association (IRATA).

There are three main levels of course:

- Level 1 Technician (Trainee) for those who want to enter the rope access industry by working for subcontractors
- Level 2 Technician (Operative) to train Level 1 workers in rigging working ropes, undertaking rescues using a variety of ropes and being able to do a range of access tasks
- Level 3 Technician (Supervisor) for those who will be responsible for supervision of rope access activities.

Most courses last five days and cost in the region of £500 but some employers pay for staff to train. The National Access and Rescue Centre offers courses approved by HSE and WAHSA.

What Else

As well as going up, rope access workers may also have to go down into ventilation shafts and hard-to-reach locations. This work might sound exciting but it is nonetheless an extremely safe career with rigorous assessment of risks, substantial training and excellent safety records, promoted and enforced by the Industrial Rope Access Trade Association (IRATA). Frequently rope access workers are employed from a contract-to-contract basis for offshore oil companies.

What It Pays

This is quite variable depending on the difficulty of access. Offshore workers can earn between £500 and £1,000 per day but for onshore work the average weekly wage might be about £324 per week.

Prospects

This is a developing career with work available in a number of different industries, including TV and media, utility companies, building/civil engineering companies and local government/authorities.

Best Advice

Get plenty of experience in abseiling/climbing/caving and decide whether you are keen enough to take qualifications in these skills. Practise! If you want to do plumbing or welding or painting and decorating, take an apprenticeship in those areas as well. Check out the IRATA website for training courses and members who might want to employ and train you.

Contacts

IRATA, Association House, Tournai Hall, Evelyn Woods Road, Aldershot, Hampshire GU11 2LL
01252 357839   www.irata.org

National Access and Rescue Centre
www.narc.co.uk

Outward Bound
www.outwardbound-uk.org

YMCA
www.ymca.org.uk

Advertising Copywriter

You can probably think of a great TV advert that always makes you laugh or one that really gets the message across in a powerful, memorable or entertaining way. While the idea of advertising as a career may be fairly familiar to you, the actual work of a copywriter may be a little less clear. In simple terms, whenever you watch, hear or read an advert, you are experiencing the work of advertising professionals who have normally worked as a team to create the idea or concept behind the advert. The copywriter, while part of this team, is primarily responsible for the words and the impact they make, whether the advert is to appear on TV/radio or in a newspaper.

Of course, the idea of creating ads for, say, a famous sporting manufacturer, using a celebrity, clever dialogue and amazing visuals, is extremely appealing. But the reality of the job may be writing newspaper 'copy' for a local funeral director or fish and chip shop. The work can vary enormously from the extremely mundane to multi-million-pound campaigns, but in essence it is always about creating the perfect mix of words to attract attention and persuade someone to 'buy' something, whether it is an idea, a product or a service.

There are, of course, many types of advertising including newspapers and magazines, directories, radio, TV, the internet and outdoor/transport sources such as buses, hoardings or even hot-air balloons. The two main sources for jobs in advertising are specialist agencies, which organise and create advertising campaigns for companies and organisations, and the media (newspapers, magazines, radio, TV, etc.), which sells advertising space or slots.

The Job Description
Copywriters are responsible for creating the words, the 'copy', that form the message or idea of the ad. They have to come up with words, phrases, slogans that fit the overall campaign idea. They have to be creative within the boundaries of the overall concept, as agreed with the client and the design team. They cannot just sit and make up whatever copy they like. They work as part of the creative team to produce the concept of the ad from the customer or client's brief, the original advertising concept, as decided at the initial consultation. A copywriter works in very close partnership with a visualiser or artist/graphic designer to define the perfect representation of what the client/company requires, according to the 'brief'. The creative team, including the writers and visualisers, may have to come up with many different approaches, which may be displayed to the customer through storyboards. These creatives have to put together a verbal and visual concept that excites the customer, and

this means that writers and visualisers must have a thorough understanding of the target market for the ad.

The Person Specification

The skill required to be a successful copywriter is based around an ability to write clearly and concisely in a number of different styles for a variety of audiences, in the most persuasive and often enticing way. It demands highly technical, honed writing skills. Copywriters have to be able to:

- come up with new ideas
- bounce ideas around within a team
- pay attention to detail
- understand market research about the target buyer
- be extremely selective and passionate about the choice of words and the levels of meaning available from the smallest phrase
- ensure that what they write does not breach the codes of advertising practice
- be rigorous about spelling, grammar and facts
- revise, amend and change copy tirelessly until it is acceptable to the client.

What It Takes

While this is a highly competitive area for jobs, it is still possible to become a copywriter on writing talent alone, as formal qualifications are not absolutely required for this job. However, good copywriters invariably have talent *and* qualifications. So further/higher-level study of some kind can be useful, whether it be a degree in business, marketing or even English or classics, a Foundation degree in advertising or a specialised writing or communication qualification. These might give you the chance to develop your writing skills to the kind of level needed, so take a look at courses that are titled 'Advertising and Marketing Communication' or 'Media Writing'.

The Institute of Copywriting offers a Diploma in Copywriting which can be studied through home study/distance learning and may take less than nine months, depending on how motivated you are. Many people take the Communication, Advertising and Marketing Education (CAM) Diploma in Marketing Communications. The Advertising Association also has a list of possible courses on their website.

However you choose to study, it will be important that you add to your experience in any way you can by getting practice in writing through work placements, vacation activities or voluntary work. You may find that a local charity would be happy to allow you to do some free work for them, designing leaflets or adverts for local papers. Examples of work you have done in a paid or unpaid capacity can then go into your portfolio or 'book', which you can use when you are applying for work. This will give proof of your ability to write in a precise and appealing way and might really give you the edge in a competitive market.

It is worth noting that many advertising agencies have well-regarded graduate training programmes, which attract hordes of applicants; selection for these trainee jobs is often through a variety of challenging assessment procedures including role play, real-world assignments, presentations and monitored/observed discussions. Once recruited though, whether as a junior straight from school/college or after a university course, training will be on the job and ongoing, possibly through additional courses such as the Institute of Practitioners in Advertising (IPA) Foundation Certificate (a work-based course).

What Else

Getting the attention of a possible employer for your first copywriting post will be like launching your own ad campaign. You will be selling the concept of yourself to advertising agencies or media companies. If you do not have the creativity to think of an interesting angle, it may be a sign that this work is not for you. Nonetheless, there are some commonsense things you can do. You will need a portfolio of your work, often called your 'book', showing eye-catching examples of ideas and concepts that you have turned into sparkling, effective copy. Present your examples of copy in a simple, striking format and let it speak for itself. If it doesn't, then it isn't good copy.

What It Pays

Pay varies across the country, but a typical starting salary would be £12,000–£17,000 per year for junior positions and £18,000–£25,000 per year for graduate roles.

Prospects

Experienced copywriters may progress onto posts as creative directors or work on a freelance basis.

Best Advice

In this extremely competitive and commercial market, high levels of undentable confidence, enormous talent, flexibility and persistence are needed. The Institute of Practitioners in Advertising (IPA) (see below) lists only 284 member agencies which tend to be the larger agencies; many agencies are small and may employ under 50 people, so it is a relatively small job market which you will be targeting.

Do your research using the excellent websites listed below. The D&AD website is particularly useful to give you a flavour of the industry and most websites have a jobs online section. Research will help you identify the agencies that you want to work for and how to pitch your applications. A direct, polite telephone approach to a named person (discovered through your painstaking research) is recommended, followed by an informal interview where you can present your book/ portfolio.

Gain any writing experience you can. Offer to write ads for a student newspaper or work for a charity fundraising campaign writing copy for free. Get involved in any kind of sideline marketing or public relations activities. Send in articles and letters to local newspapers or fanzines. Keep copies of your successes.

Many good university courses include a placement with an ad agency and this is a great opportunity to impress. Many placement students get offered graduate jobs on the strength of placement success.

Finally, if you manage by sheer persistence and courtesy to gain access to an advertising director, beg advice and feedback on your portfolio, negotiate a work placement of even a few days' duration and make yourself so indispensable that they offer you more work. This might just result in a real contract. Realise that a first job will probably include quite a bit of dogsbody work and you might have to start early and work late to show your keenness.

Contacts

The Advertising Association, 7th Floor North, Artillery House, 11–19 Artillery Row, London SW1P 1RT
020 7340 1100   www.adassoc.org.uk

The Institute of Practitioners in Advertising, 44 Belgrave Square, London SW1X 8QS
020 7235 7020   www.ipa.co.uk

Communication, Advertising and Marketing Education Foundation Ltd (CAM)
www.camfoundation.com

D&AD
www.dandad.org

Arboriculturalist/Arborist

Arboriculturalists or aborists are tree experts and they spend their time planting and caring for trees and shrubs in recreational, woodland or urban areas. They may be called tree surgeons or arborists, but the job involves quite a bit more than chopping down dangerous branches of trees. They are experts on tree and plant propagation, tree diseases and improving the environment.

The Job Description
Arboriculturalists are responsible for woodland landscaping. This might mean that they work for some of their time in a tree nursery, raising plants from seedlings. They might work with landscape architects or local authority planners to plant trees to improve the environment. They might develop new areas of woodland and be involved in the conservation of trees. As part of their job, it might be necessary to climb trees using safety harnesses to prune leaves and branches. Other job titles in this work may be tree surgeon or arboricultural officer for a local authority. As a tree surgeon you might have to climb trees for a living (to heights of up to 36 metres), using a chainsaw to prune or fell trees.

The Person Specification
At one level, arboriculturalists are keen environmentalists and are committed to working in the environment, whether that's a city centre or a country park. They act as advisers on tree resource management and tree siting. They also advise on the effects of construction work on trees. They may have to recommend the felling of trees in difficult or dangerous positions. On another level, this is an active outdoor job so they need to be physically fit, agile and prepared to be outdoors in all weathers. They have to like climbing trees, and have to know how to do this in the safest possible way. An arboriculturalist needs to be:

- able to work within health and safety regulations
- able to climb trees
- happy working at great heights
- able to follow plans and diagrams
- familiar with the science of trees, habitats and pests and diseases associated with trees
- able to work well in a team with other horticultural/landscape colleagues
- careful using pesticides and chemicals.

What It Takes

Many horticultural colleges offer National Certificate/Diploma courses, lasting 2–3 years, in Amenity Design or Landscape Design which cover aspects of arboriculture; normally four GCSE passes, C grade and over, or equivalent, including maths, English and a science, are required for entry to these courses. These courses may lead on to diploma/certificate or Foundation degree courses in arboriculture. It may be possible to take an apprenticeship with a landscape firm or local authority and learn on the job, taking NVQs in horticulture or arboriculture. This might lead to jobs with arboricultural or tree surgery firms.

There are specialist courses in arboriculture, which can only normally be taken after an initial horticultural training course, and are accredited by the Arboricultural Association or the Royal Forestry Society. At the highest level, there are also university degrees and postgraduate courses in Forestry, which cover arboriculture.

Colleges/universities and the Arboricultural Association will advise you on the recommended qualifications, set down by health and safety regulations, which you will need to pass to be able to work on trees, particularly for the tree surgery side of the work. At the most basic level you will need a chainsaw certification as a legal requirement. You may also need to be trained in the safe use of pesticides. The Arboricultural Association's own Technician Certificate in Arboriculture is highly regarded and is proof of technical competence and safe working practices.

What Else

Arboriculturalists work for local authorities, woodland contractors and landscape firms. In the summer, working hours tend to be longer, including work at weekends and in the evening. If you have hay fever or are allergic to certain chemicals, this may not be the job for you.

What It Pays

Once trained and qualified, arboricultural workers normally earn in the region of £16,000–£18,000 per year but experienced and qualified climbing arborists can earn from £20,000–£29,000 per year.

Prospects

It is possible to work on a self-employed basis, or for the Forestry Commission, or for large estates with substantial woodland. Once fully experienced, you may be able to work in a supervisory capacity, negotiating and planning work to be done.

Best Advice

The Arboricultural Association has excellent information on its website including details about approved contractors and their own training courses. They even have tree-climbing competitions.

Contacts

The Arboricultural Association, Ampfield House, Romsey, Hampshire SO51 9PA
01794 368717   www.trees.org.uk

The Forestry Commission, 231 Corstorphine Road, Edinburgh EH12 7AT
0131 314 6379   www.forestry.gov.uk

Royal Forestry Society
www.rfs.org.uk

Archivist

In simple terms, an archive is a collection of records, probably of historical significance, and so an archivist is someone who is in charge of preserving, recording and organising all kinds of materials or items that it contains. This can sound fascinating or extremely dull according to where your interests lie. You could be working for a government department, your local city or county council, a church, hospital, museum, a college or a business.

The Job Description

As an archivist, you would be responsible for organising the archives to preserve past records including manuscripts, books, documents, maps, photographs, film or computer-generated records, which need to be kept permanently for the future. Your job would be to ensure that these records are classified, indexed or catalogued in a way that makes the information easy for someone else to access at any time. You might be responsible for acquiring new items or records, talking with owners of artefacts, and negotiating purchases or loans. You might also assist visitors who want to use the archive for research. You might help out with exhibitions or give presentations for local community or business groups. You may also help interpret particular archives for archive users and make decisions on what should be preserved or retained.

You would probably be based in a record office or specialist museum or repository, although you might also be involved in rescuing records from unusual locations such as disused buildings.

The Person Specification

The kind of person who would like this work is interested in heritage information management in general, that is preserving often irreplaceable, even priceless resources for future generations. You would need to be:

- interested in history
- a good communicator, especially to help visitors use the archive
- prepared to use computers and technology to preserve archive items
- logical and organised
- interested in research
- accurate and able to pay attention to often minute detail.

What It Takes

You will need a degree and/or postgraduate qualification, preferably in a subject like archive and museum studies, history, librarianship and/ or information science, a language, classics or something similar. Many entrants to this job choose to take an undergraduate or postgraduate qualification recognised by the Society of Archivists – these are listed on their website. As there are a limited number of accredited courses, competition for places is intense, and most successful applicants have been involved in some 'hands-on' paid or volunteer experience in archive work to help increase their chances.

What Else

Almost half the archivists employed in the UK are employed in local government (county or city councils); others may work for national archives or, increasingly, businesses. It is also possible to work abroad as an archivist in Europe, America or Australasia.

What It Pays

Local government archivists are likely to start on £17,000–£24,000 per year, with business and specialist archives paying varying rates of pay. The Society of Archivists recommends a minimum salary of £20,295 per year.

Prospects

This is a small and somewhat specialist area of work. Most new entrants to this work start as assistant archivists on short-term contracts with possible progression to more senior roles through experience. Being prepared to move about the country is important if you want to extend your career and expertise in this work.

Best Advice

Some organisations/institutions offer one-year paid graduate traineeships and many offer unpaid work experience. The Society of Archivists lists and advertises traineeships. Become a student member of the Society of Archivists and you will have access to job information and current discussion topics for archivists.

Try and visit some local archives to see what they are like; even research a topic with the help of an archivist. Contact the Society of Archivists to arrange a work experience placement within an archive office.

Contacts

Society of Archivists, Prioryfield House, 20 Cannon Street, Taunton, Somerset TA1 1SW
01823 327077   www.archives.org.uk

Art Therapist

Art therapists work with people with mental, emotional, medical or physical problems, helping patients to express their feelings artistically or creatively. This kind of therapy can be used to relieve stress or anxiety and to help people communicate better, so that health professionals, who may be psychiatrists or medical consultants, can decide on the best treatment for individual patients.

Typically, an art therapist may set up a creative setting using simple art materials like paint or clay and allow patients to express their feelings in a non-verbal way; this allows medical professionals to understand the patient better and make better evaluations for further treatment.

The Job Description

Art therapists work with adults or children in community-based centres, child-guidance clinics, prisons, hospitals and for social services. Their role is not to teach people to be artistic, but to use the most suitable type of visual art or creative activity to help bring patients out of themselves enough to aid a self-healing process. They have to be able to assess people who need therapy and determine the best course of action to help the person manage their situation. For example, they may use simple watercolour painting with a young child who has suffered abuse; the process of producing the artwork may act as a form of release for the child, and help health or social services professionals deal with the situation in the best way possible. In many cases, the artwork or pottery or craft work can be used as a useful aid to diagnosis of a mental health problem or repressed feelings. Art therapists work on a one-to-one basis or with a small group of patients.

Art therapists may also be called craft instructors, hobby therapists, teachers or tutors, and they have to work closely with psychologists, psychiatrists, social workers and community workers. Art is used as a way of relieving frustration and can reduce the effects of certain disabilities; it has an important part to play in helping people get over severe illnesses or in helping them come to terms with permanent health problems.

The Person Specification

For this kind of work, you would need to have a strong interest in art in all its forms and a real motivation to help others to use creativity to communicate their problems or pain. Sensitivity towards adults and children, without over-involvement, is needed, as well as an ability to work in a therapeutic setting with individuals or groups. You would need:

- artistic ability and empathy
- creativity in an artistic sense, as well as in finding solutions to problems
- emotional stability, including being able to recognise your own strengths and weaknesses
- flexibility in being able to deal with a variety of situations
- an interest in psychological processes.

What It Takes

This is a relatively small and rare profession, with many health workers doing this type of work either as part of their job or without the job title 'art therapist'. It seems to be a growing profession, as it has gained acceptance as a valuable therapeutic tool, particularly in the USA, where it is estimated that about 5,000 art therapists are employed. However, the numbers employed in this country are smaller but on the increase – the British Association of Art Therapists (BAAT) has 1,200 qualified members and around 250 trainees. As a result competition for jobs is intense, with often only under five jobs per month advertised on the BAAT website to members.

Firstly, you would need to be a graduate in art or design/fine art/ community arts, or a qualified health professional, teacher or therapist, and then you could apply for the postgraduate diploma courses in art therapy or art psychotherapy.

To work as an art therapist in the National Health Service or in social services, you need a postgraduate diploma in art therapy or art psychotherapy, which is accredited by BAAT. This qualification is also recognised in the USA and Europe and would allow you to apply for Health Professions Council registration, which is compulsory to practise as an art therapist in the UK.

Occasionally, graduates from social sciences or humanities courses may be offered places on BAAT accredited courses. Occupational therapists, psychiatric nurses, teachers and social workers may also apply for the postgraduate diploma. In addition, applicants for diploma courses will be expected to have at least 6–12 months' suitable work experience and possibly a portfolio of artwork.

What Else

BAAT offer short courses such as the Introduction to the Profession of Art Therapy and the Art Therapy Foundation course as a way for graduates to learn about art therapy in more depth.

Voluntary or paid work experience in any care setting is recommended. You will need to show evidence of interpersonal qualities, as well as artistic skills for entry to this career. Try and get to meet an art therapist or someone in a similar role and contact BAAT for further information.

What It Pays

Pay varies according to type of employment, as some art therapists are employed by the NHS who pay on a particular pay scale, while others may work for social services or are self-employed. Self-employed or sessional work is increasingly common. Part-time work is also possible. Hours of work are generally 9–5 with some travelling between bases. Starting salaries are likely to be £20,970 per year for NHS work.

Prospects

Increasingly, art therapists work on a session-by-session basis for more than one employer. This might involve work in a prison, a day centre, a school support centre or a hospital. There are even some employment options for self-employment work as a private practitioner.

Best Advice

Check out the BAAT journal *Inscape* for useful background information and advertised vacancies.

Contacts

British Association of Art Therapists, 24–27 White Lion Street, London N1 9PD
020 7686 4216   www.baat.org

NHS Careers
www.nhscareers.nhs.uk

Audiologist/Audiology Technician

This is one of those less well-known career which is, nonetheless, an important and often fascinating job, working within the National Health Service (NHS). Audiology is also a developing field that offers someone the chance to work in a scientific/technical job that helps and supports people in a real and rewarding way.

The Job Description

Audiologists work with patients to determine and assess hearing or problems connected with balance. They will also get involved in using equipment which measures sound and hearing capacity and be responsible for fitting both simple hearing aids and complex cochlear implants.

Audiology technicians (who are graded as medical technical officers/medical physics technicians in the NHS) assist audiologists and help to diagnose and treat hearing loss or balance disorders. They use equipment to measure and assess someone's hearing (this could be a child or an adult) and diagnose specific hearing conditions. They might also help someone adjust to their hearing problem and fit hearing aids, offering support and encouragement.

The Person Specification

Audiologists and audiology technicians work closely with patients and need to be sensitive when using the, sometimes, strange-looking technical equipment, which might seem rather off-putting to patients. They have to take the time to care for this audiometric equipment. Working in hospitals or clinics, they are part of a medical team but they also have to be able to work on their own, taking responsibility for particular patients.

While technicians might be involved in routine testing of patients and find themselves working under the supervision of a trained audiologist, audiologists take the full responsibility for their patient caseload and make referrals to other medical health professionals, depending on their assessment of the need. For this job you would need to be:

- good with technical equipment and people
- calm, sensitive and encouraging
- prepared to understand the realities of each patient's daily life
- interested in health.

What It Takes

Technician level – interestingly, for this career you can go into the job as a medical technical officer trainee, starting as a technician and training on the job, so previous experience or training is not necessary. Most hospitals or clinics recruit staff with GCSE passes (or equivalent) in maths, English and science. Any experience in a caring role, either as a volunteer or in paid work, would be considered useful. The NHS often offers training through day release to a local college for the BTEC in Medical Physics or Physiological Measurement. These courses cover maths, physics, medical instrumentation and human physiology. It is also possible to carry on with this training through university level courses and be paid by the NHS up to MSc level, when a technician would progress to being a professional audiologist.

Audiologist level – you may decide to take the more direct route and take a degree in audiology or postgraduate training after an initial science degree. The degree takes four years and involves substantial real experience through a clinical placement in the third year. There are only nine universities in the UK offering these courses and these are listed on the NHS website. Many science graduates apply for funded postgraduate training through the NHS Clinical Scientists scheme.

What Else

Audiology is non-invasive diagnostic work, but you will need to be comfortable with people who might be upset or concerned about their health condition. You could be dealing with babies or small children, adults with hearing loss or those with learning or physical disabilities and high-level people skills are needed, such as empathy and a caring attitude. In addition, you would have to stay objective and analytical to be able to assess accurately the data produced by the audiological equipment.

Currently the NHS pays bursaries for training in audiology, and tuition fees are also covered. This means less student debt for UK students.

What It Pays

Starting salaries for NHS audiology technicians are in the region of £17,000–£20,000 per year and for audiologists the pay scale is £22,000–£31,000 per year.

Prospects

Further study for audiology technicians to degree level and beyond opens up better career opportunities. Audiologists often branch off into research work.

Best Advice

Work hard at biology, chemistry and physics – all of these sciences are used in audiological careers. Many hospitals have a volunteer programme, which would give you the chance to experience a hospital environment and give you valuable experience for your CV and university applications. Any volunteering with children with hearing impairment or sign-language training would also be useful. Most colleges offer evening classes in British Sign Language.

Contacts

British Academy of Audiology, Association House, South Park Road, Macclesfield, Cheshire SK11 6SH
01625 504066   www.baaudiology.org

British Society of Audiology, 80 Brighton Road, Reading, Berkshire RG6 1PS
0118 966 0622   www.thebsa.org.uk

NHS Careers
www.nhscareers.nhs.uk

Clinical Scientist Training Scheme
www.nhsclinicalscientists.info/clr/recruitment

Betting Analyst

A betting analyst is responsible for managing bets placed by gamblers in betting shops, at racecourses or on the internet so that predictions can be made and, ultimately, sports betting organisations do not lose money. It may seem unlikely that any accurate predictions could be made on the success or failure of a football game or a horserace, but analysts make use of detailed data and complex calculations to ensure that the risk of a big loss is prevented. Large sports betting organisations rely on the expertise of betting analysts to make the right decision about a bet in a high-pressure situation.

The Job Description
Betting analysts use the latest statistical analysis techniques and a network of contacts to derive the most up-to-date and accurate predictions possible for sport throughout the world. They manage and control betting, the odds and the customers by analysing betting patterns and making price changes accordingly. They may have to liaise with customers, analyse data and make reports and recommendations to senior traders who make the final decisions. It helps if they have a strong interest in sport and knowledge of spread betting or the bookmaking industry.

The Person Specification
In-depth training is needed for this job, but a suitable candidate would be someone who wants to work in a high-pressure business where quick judgements and attention to detail are vital. You would need to be:

- highly numerate, as calculating bets is a key part of the role
- a good communicator – with customers over the phone or with other colleagues
- able to act decisively
- flexible and able to deal with several things at once
- really interested in, and knowledgeable about, sport, gambling and betting
- analytical and logical in order to help select value bets.

What It Takes
Most trainee roles recruit graduates of any degree course, but degree subjects with strong numerical or statistical focus would be considered particularly useful. Salford University (www.salford.ac.uk) offers a degree in Gambling and Leisure Management which may be valuable for entry to this work. To study for a relevant degree you would need to have a good GCSE profile or equivalent, with C grades and over in maths, English and

science, while A levels/Diploma level in subjects such as maths/statistics, law or business may be helpful.

It may be possible to start off working in a large betting-shop chain after A levels/Diploma, and then take an in-company career route to this work. You need to be at least 18 years old to work in a betting shop.

What Else

If a particular customer is regularly beating the betting company, then analysts will take note and make betting price changes on the basis of the predicted success of this customer.

What It Pays

Starting salaries for major companies are around £29,000 per year.

Prospects

There are various career progression jobs with sports betting companies including work as a senior trader or work at racecourses or odds compiling for different sports; there are also opportunities to work on strange, unusual or long-range betting forecast analysis such as the chances of snow falling on Christmas Day or a particular team making it through to a championship.

Best Advice

Learning is constant in this career and a wide knowledge of sport and economics in general is vital for this job role, so keep current by reading the newspapers and specialist papers such as the *Racing Post*. Get some experience as soon as you are 18 years of age with a bookmakers' shop.

Contacts

Gambling Commission, Victoria Square House, Victoria Square, Birmingham B2 4BP
0121 230 6666   www.gamblingcommission.gov.uk

National Association of Bookmakers, PO Box 242, East Molesey, Surrey KT8 2WE
01884 841859   http://nab-bookmakers.co.uk

Betting Jobs
www.bettingjobs.com

Biomedical Scientist (BMS)

Biomedical science (BMS) is about how the body actually works, how disease affects it, and through BMS research, trying to find cures for illness and disease. Within BMS, there are many specialisms, such as microbiology, transfusion science and histopathology.

The Job Description

Without BMS there would be no scientific diagnosis of illness, no treatment and no research into causes and cures for disease. Doctors decide on the best treatment for their patients based on the results these scientists produce. The support role they offer is vital, as it is they who carry out tests on human samples to determine treatment, identify blood groups and analyse cultures, monitor medication and observe treatment. They work with an extraordinary range of medical conditions such as AIDS, cancer, hepatitis, diabetes and cervical smears. Most of the work is laboratory based but computers and high-tech equipment play a significant part in their analytical work.

The Person Specification

This is a strong analytical and scientific career based in hospitals, research laboratories or medical research units. To do this job you would need to be:

- both confident and highly competent in sciences, particularly chemistry and biology
- interested in health and the prevention of disease
- analytical and logical
- a good record keeper
- accurate and highly attentive to detail
- able to gather and weigh up data
- determined and committed
- able to work under pressure to provide results of tests within urgent time deadlines.

What It Takes

A broad range of GCSE passes (grade C and above) or equivalent, including maths, English and sciences, would be a good start, followed by A levels/Diploma or equivalent in biology and chemistry or health sciences. You would then need to undertake a biomedical science degree or similar. The National Health Service recruits graduate scientists for BMS Medical Laboratory Scientific Officer (MLSO) training and would train you through to state registration.

What Else

Biomedical scientists can work beyond the NHS for pharmaceutical companies, the Blood Transfusion Service, the Medical Research Council, the Health and Safety Executive and the World Health Organization. The nature of biomedical-type tasks means that some of the work can be routine and painstaking, but the need for accuracy and efficiency is paramount.

What It Pays

NHS starting salaries for Health Professions Council (HPC) state-registered scientists are around £18,000–20,000 per year.

Prospects

There is a clear pay and career structure offered by the NHS which includes ongoing training. Overseas work is a likely possibility for a qualified biomedical scientist. The work they do is often at the cutting edge of research so career progression is possible and probable within different specialisms.

Best Advice

Check the NHS website for further information on biomedical scientist careers.

King's College, London (www.kcl.ac.uk), which provides one of the specialised biomedical science degree courses, runs various summer schools each year for Year 11 students, which would be an interesting way to find out more about the job and the courses available. Work hard at your sciences – you will need them.

Contacts

Institute of Biomedical Science, 12 Coldbath Square, London EC1R 5HL
020 7713 0214   www.ibms.org

Health Professions Council (HPC), Park House, 184 Kennington Park Road, London SE11 4BU
020 7582 0866   www.hpc-uk.org

NHS Careers
www.nhscareers.nhs.uk

Brand Protection Manager

If you've ever bought something fake and regretted it later, then you might realise how important it can be to know that you're buying the real deal. When something falls apart or doesn't work later, it's because the quality of a brand has not been protected. Brand protection is part of a commercial strategy to ensure that customers are not exploited and that the reputation of an established brand is safeguarded.

The Job Description

A brand protection manager is responsible for protecting the intellectual property rights and brand interests of a company from infringements by third parties, who might be rogue traders making money by trading on the brand name of a well-known company. They generally work for large or even multinational companies who need to protect their image and reputation in global markets. The work of a brand protection manager can include registering trade marks, maintaining the trade-mark portfolio and anti-counterfeiting activity, such as carrying out investigations which could involve potentially risky raids and seizures of counterfeit or illegal merchandise.

The work can be office based for registering of trade marks, legal activities and checking of fraudulent internet activity, or out and about for enforcement raids, seizures and training of enforcement officials, such as customs and trading standards officers.

The Person Specification

A brand protection manager will be tasked with being proactive in seeking out those who infringe intellectual property (a company's ideas, brands, logos) via manufacturing, importing or selling counterfeit merchandise. To do this job, you would need to develop:

- organisational skills to plan the work undertaken
- communication skills to liaise with a range of contacts and train enforcement officials
- an ability to take the initiative and decide on a course of action
- financial skills to cost out work that needs to be done with regard to registrations and enforcement action throughout the world
- investigative skills, to track and uncover illegal activity.

What It Takes

The most usual way to move into this work is either from a legal background following a law degree which includes aspects on intellectual property, or through a consumer protection degree. Consumer protection degrees could be a route into trading standards work for a local authority and with experience this could lead into commercial jobs in brand protection. Some people start working in marketing or product development and, after gaining experience, apply for jobs in brand protection. To study for a law or marketing or consumer protection degree you would need to have a good GCSE profile or equivalent, with C grades and over in maths, English and science and A levels/Diploma in subjects such as law, business or even science.

What Else
A good grasp of law, in particular connected to trade marks, copyright and patents, is needed. Working hours can be long and some work can be dangerous (working on markets with trading standards/police or raid action) and weekend work may also be required.

What It Pays
As this is a managerial post with considerable responsibility, salaries start at around £30,000.

Prospects
There are restricted numbers of vacancies within this line of work as it is specialist and often undercover by its nature. However, other work in consumer protection may be possible. Consultancy and other brand awareness management roles or higher level general management roles may also be possible.

Best Advice
Research brands and the ideas behind the concept of intellectual property. Build up an interest and knowledge in brand and product/service. Try and gain work experience with major brands. Get some legal experience and consider consumer protection degrees – see UCAS www.ucas.com for courses.

Contacts
Trading Standards Institute, Sylvan Court, Sylvan Way, Southfields Business Park, Basildon, Essex SS15 6TH
0870 872 9000   www.tsi.org.uk

Anti Counterfeiting Group
www.a-cg.com

Brewer

For some people, the idea of being a brewer ranks along with chocolate taster as a highly desirable occupation. Although most breweries have tasting sessions for quality control, the job is more about the technical, highly scientific production process that turns malt, barley, hops and yeast into beer. A brewer may be called a technical brewer or process/production manager and will be responsible for the automated process that makes beer to a consistent quality and taste.

The Job Description

The brewer can be on the production floor, working with operators, equipment and machinery which turn the raw materials into beer. They could also be responsible for managing raw materials, talking to people in the laboratory about test results, scheduling the whole brewing process and ensuring the overall quality of the product. Depending on the size of the brewery, they may be in a more production-based role or a more technical role or a mixture of the two.

Brewers have a knowledge of biochemistry and perhaps of mechanical or chemical engineering in order to control the production process which goes to make beer or alcohol. They may test samples at various stages, checking for the strength and taste of the beer, and make adjustments when necessary. They may specialise in one stage of the process like fermentation or quality control, but in essence this is a scientific job as well as a management role.

The Person Specification

Brewers are managers of the production process, so they have to be able to cope with plant or machinery problems and supervise technicians and operators. You would need to be:

- interested in science, particularly chemistry
- numerate and computer literate
- good with people
- able to pay attention to detail
- good with machinery.

What It Takes

Most brewers have a degree in brewing/distilling, chemistry, biochemistry, food science or chemical engineering. You would need A levels in chemistry, biology and maths or physics or a Diploma in sciences. Heriot Watt University in Scotland hosts the International Centre for Brewing and Distilling and offers a BSc degree in Brewing and Distilling. Trainee brewers who enter graduate training with brewing companies normally study for Associate Membership of the Institute of Brewing (IOB) and then take the Institute of Brewing Diploma in Brewing or Distilling.

What Else

The Diploma Master Brewer examination of the IOB is the highest technical standard and the one most brewers aim for, if they want to have good job opportunities in the brewing industry.

What It Pays

Large brewing companies have graduate training schemes that recruit people from university courses, with starting salaries being around £16,000–£24,000 per year. Head brewers can earn between £42,000 and £65,000 per year.

Prospects

This is a small profession so competition for jobs is strong. Be sure to consider both the large and smaller brewers for possible career openings.

Best Advice

Try and organise a visit to a brewery from school or college. It may be possible to try work experience as a way of checking this out. Some distilleries in Scotland offer paid vacation work.

Contacts

The Institute of Brewing, 33 Clarges Street, London W1Y 7EE
020 7499 8144   www.ibd.org.uk

International Centre for Brewing and Distilling (ICBD)
www.icbd.hw.ac.uk

Broadcast Engineer

Working for a TV or radio station seems pretty appealing to most people but you do not need to be in front of the camera – you can work in a number of technical areas and one of these is the role of broadcast engineer. Broadcast engineers are responsible for a range of technical processes that really make programmes happen. If you can imagine the whole array of studio equipment and systems which result in a programme transmission, then you can probably understand how important the engineers are in the scheme of things. They install systems, set up links for outside broadcasts and monitor constantly for problems which might cause one of those blank screen moments for the TV viewer.

The Job Description

The term 'broadcast engineer' actually describes a person skilled in a whole range of technical areas, from someone who is a set electrician to someone who repairs or maintains hardware or software for interactive media. Engineers may be listed as 'best boy' in the credits of a programme and, though these engineers certainly do not have to be boys, they often have to be best at what they do. They will have to deal with routine and difficult situations which ultimately are crucial for broadcasting because, without their expertise, no television or radio programme would happen. So anything technical, electrical, electronic or computer related will be their responsibility; they could be based in a studio or in a van for an outside broadcast. They might be testing, monitoring or servicing equipment, or installing systems from scratch. They could be operating the satellite van, taking calls about faults or safety testing.

The Person Specification

Broadcast engineers need to be fairly multi-skilled but normally have expertise in electrical/electronic, computer or specifically broadcast engineering. You would need to be:

- a practical/technical kind of person
- fascinated by broadcasting, whether radio, TV, podcasts or other interactive media
- keen to be current with new technologies and their uses
- pretty comfortable with IT and all its uses
- able to be flexible and work as part of a team
- prepared to work long and unsocial hours at times.

What It Takes
It may be possible to train as an electrician through an apprenticeship (after GCSE passes at C grade and over or equivalent in maths, English and science at least) and gain entry to a set electrician scheme with a TV or film company, but most people take university degrees in broadcast engineering, electrical/electronic engineering or similar and then try to get first jobs with broadcast companies. For degree/Foundation degree study you would need a GCSE or equivalent profile of maths, English, science and a technology subject at C grade or over, and A levels/ Diploma, probably including maths and/or physics.

Competition for graduate or entry jobs is fierce so any experience additional to this that you can offer will be vital. You might try working for hospital radio as a volunteer or work for free in local radio or in a recording studio. The BBC broadcast engineering training scheme, which is highly regarded, takes applications from time to time – look out for it at www.bbc.co.uk/jobs. Otherwise check major TV and radio websites on a regular basis for trainee vacancies. Some people start as runners (see page 185).

What Else
Advances in broadcasting technology make this an exciting career with constant changes and developments. Early morning starts (4.30a.m.), particularly in radio, are extremely common, so you need to be a morning person.

What It Pays
Starting salaries are in the range £16,000–£18,000 per year.

Prospects
You will probably be working for a major employer such as the well-known terrestrial and digital TV channels or for production/post-production companies or studios. You may be able to move into higher technical roles requiring greater expertise and experience or into specialisation with regard to specific equipment or areas of broadcast.

Best Advice
Research this career carefully, checking on TV and radio websites for typical vacancies. Get the best overall training possible and take any opportunity you can to gain real experience through work experience in local or hospital radio. Be prepared to compete hard for jobs – you will need to be determined. The FT2 scheme, sponsored by film and TV companies, offers an annual technical training scheme which would be ideal as a way into this work. The two-year training offers four separate six-month paid placements with film or TV companies.

Contacts

Skillset, Focus Point, 21 Caledonian Road, London N1 9GB
020 7713 9800   www.skillset.org/careers

BBC
www.bbc.co.uk/talent or www.bbc.co.uk/workexperience

Channel 4
www.channel4.com/4careers

FT2
www.ft2.org.uk

Child Protection Officer (CPO)

Child protection is a core aspect of a number of caring professions, but social workers, who have a primary duty of care and a legal obligation to protect children from harm, are often considered the experts in this area. Child protection officers are often employed by county, borough and city council social services departments and they have a special responsibility for the welfare of children. It is, in fact, one area of specialism possible for social workers and has links with fostering and adoption, the care of children involved in divorce proceedings or those suffering mental health problems. CPOs also work with young people who leave care or children's homes, and undertake family support work.

The government is committed to positive outcomes for children and young people, and child protection work is concerned with preventing anything getting in the way of a child's right to grow, develop and feel safe. Most people would recognise the importance of child protection, but only a very few would find that they have the qualities, skills and emotional robustness to work with families and children who may be experiencing serious difficulties. Idealism might tempt you to this job, but to work effectively and cope with the grim realities of the role, you would need to be much more than idealistic.

The Job Description

Child protection officers are qualified social workers who are employed by local government, social services or specific childcare charities to support and protect children at risk. They have a duty to intervene if they suspect a child is being harmed, but they also need to pick up on clues to prevent abuse occurring in the first place. As you can imagine, this is an extremely challenging job and a CPO has the power to remove a child from a family situation if they suspect any harm might occur. This is a very serious decision to make, especially when information gathered can sometimes seem confusing or inconclusive.

While the job role might seem to be about prevention and action in cases of child abuse, CPOs also advise organisations such as the police and schools/colleges on the best procedures for safeguarding children.

The Person Specification

A CPO may have a caseload of children to assess, and may receive referrals requesting assessment of risk for a particular child. Visits to the family and advice on managing the situation, whether it concerns a child's behaviour or helping parents know how to deal with their own troubled lives, might result from an initial referral. To do this job, you would need to be:

- interested in children and able to encourage children to trust you
- keen to help and support families
- willing to take tough decisions
- able to investigate objectively
- extremely organised and accurate about record keeping
- a good communicator
- able to work with other social workers and agencies to support your work.

What It Takes

There is currently only one way to train to be a social worker in this country, and that is through a degree in social work, which will take you three years of university study – see www.socialworkcareers.co.uk for lists of accredited courses. This involves learning about the theory of caring for people, sociology and psychology, and time spent on placement in social care situations to gain real-world experience. To gain a place on a degree in social work, you will probably need good GCSE passes (C grade and over) or equivalent, including English and maths and A levels/Diploma or equivalent, and experience of paid or voluntary caring work. Currently there are social work bursaries of about £4,000 per year to encourage students to train for social work.

Remember that regardless of qualifications you gain, you will need to show the personal qualities and skills needed to cope with the demands of this job.

What Else

There are many ways to test out whether this kind of work is for you. Community Service Volunteers offer short placements with care-related projects and this would provide you with valuable experience for university or job applications. Organisations such as Barnardos, NSPCC and Sure Start offer support to 'at risk' families and children and may offer voluntary or paid support-worker jobs that could lead onto social work training. You will need to go through a Criminal Records Bureau (CRB) check to be allowed to work with children in a voluntary or paid capacity.

What It Pays

CPOs earn in the range of £19,000–£30,000 per year, depending on the responsibilities of the role.

Prospects

Currently, there are staff shortages of qualified social workers who can fulfil a child protection role, so employment prospects are good for suitably experienced applicants.

Best Advice
Any kind of volunteering with children or families, with the NSPCC or Barnardos, or with playschemes, will be valuable in helping you enter this work.

Contacts
General Social Care Council, Goldings House, 2 Hay's Lane, London
SE1 2HB
020 7397 5800   www.gscc.org.uk

Social Care and Social Work Careers Information website
www.socialworkcareers.co.uk

Community Service Volunteers
www.csv.org.uk

Sure Start
www.surestart.gov.uk

Chocolate Taster

This may sound like your dream job. However, there really is someone in every food production process who ultimately has to taste the product, so being a chocolate taster is, in fact, a real job (although it may have a less interesting job title like 'Product Development Manager' or even 'Quality Controller').

The Job Description
This job is part of a food technology process which aims to produce a perfect, consistent product. Although many of us may claim that we could do this job without any knowledge or skill, it is in fact a highly skilled job requiring extensive training and a high level of technical and scientific ability. At various stages of the production process, small batch samples of chocolate will be made up and tested by a panel of tasters, who may just be members of the public. As part of quality control, further tests for taste, texture and nutritional value will take place. Tasting is therefore an integral and highly scientific part of the production process.

The Person Specification
Most people who do this job have come into it through a food science/ technology, nutritionist or technical route and, as a result, would be expected to have strong analytical and observational skills, as well as an ability to record information in an accurate way. However, essentially you would need:

- excellent powers of taste as well as smell, as you cannot actually taste anything without a keen sense of smell
- to be able to distinguish flavour and quality and be passionate about chocolate as a product
- to be able to undertake administrative paperwork and market research to back up your taste findings
- to organise taste panels of volunteer tasters or set up testing sessions in supermarkets.

It's even been found that too much chocolate tasting can saturate your taste buds so much that you might lose the ability to assess flavour. Typically though, as a chocolate taster you might have to taste 300–500g of chocolate a day, but it's not just about munching away madly. You will also be involved in tasting new blends and developing new products.

What It Takes
Most people who go into this work have a scientific background in food technology, food science or in chemistry. The chief chocolate taster ('Sensory Evaluation Manager') at Cadbury's started his career as an

analytical chemist and moved into this work after about 10 years' related experience in the food industry. You will need to gain a degree in food science/technology or chemistry-based subjects. Many food-related university courses include work placements within the food industry for vital work experience. A levels/Diploma or equivalent in sciences, preferably including chemistry and biology, maths or physics, are normally required.

It may be possible to gain a post as a technician with a food company and progress to this type of career through an internal promotion route.

What Else

Jobs are going to be limited in chocolate tasting as there are only a few opportunities with chocolate production and food companies. It would certainly be worth offering yourself as a volunteer taste-panel tester for a chocolate production company, as this might get your taste buds' training off to a head start.

It would be wise to research food science/technology courses at universities and check whether they have placements set up with leading chocolate companies.

What It Pays

Starting salaries with food companies for graduate entrants are at the £15,000–£20,000 per year level, but experienced managers may earn £25,000–£45,000 per year.

Prospects

Product development managers can move into other marketing or management roles or into research and development and product distribution.

Best Advice

This is not necessarily a job for chocoholics, so do your research first.

Contacts

Contact your favourite chocolate company to learn more about jobs in chocolate production.

The Institute of Food Science and Technology, 5 Cambridge Court, 210 Shepherd's Bush Road, London W6 7NJ
020 7603 6313   www.ifst.org

Coastguard

Coastguards are responsible for shipping activity around the coastline of Britain, providing information to ships on weather and tides, monitoring radio messages and calling for support from lifeboat services, helicopters or the police when necessary. They are employed by the Maritime and Coastguard Agency and provide information to the government, individuals and the media on anything to do with navigation, shipping and marine safety.

The Job Description

Coastguard watch assistants work mainly indoors at rescue centres, co-ordinating information about shipping activities. They deal with radio messages from ships about weather and tides, and take distress calls and supervise rescue teams, responding to maritime agencies on a 24-hour basis. They have to keep detailed logs about weather conditions and shipping activity in their area.

Coastguard watch officers are based in an operations centre, supervising search and rescue activities and investigating illegal operations. They may also get involved with cliff rescues, coastal searches and rescue work at sea.

The Person Specification

Coastguards have to use good judgement to analyse information received, which might be pollution reports, coastal erosion data or information about illegal smuggling. They have to be responsible and reliable, with a general knowledge of communications and navigation. You would need to be:

- able to work as part of a team
- ready to take a leadership role, when necessary
- physically fit
- able to communicate clearly and give instructions precisely, often by radio or telephone
- able to write reports, keep accurate logs and have good IT skills
- able to follow charts, graphs and tables to monitor weather, sea conditions and shipping movements
- able to stay calm under pressure or dangerous situations
- able to make quick decisions and think quickly.

What It Takes

A coastguard watch assistant is basically an administrative role, so administrative experience/and or qualifications are usual. You will need good literacy and numeracy, and keyboard/computing skills. You will also need a clear speaking voice.

Coastguard watch officers are generally recruited from a Royal Navy/ Merchant Navy or extensive sea experience background.

It is possible to apply for work as a coastguard rescue officer volunteer and be trained to deal with emergencies and basic rescues. You would be paid simply for the hours you work and this is dependent on you living close to an operational centre and the work being available. You would just be called upon, as and when needed, and if there was a particular crisis or incident. This is a good route into gaining the experience to apply for watch officer roles.

What Else

You would be employed by HM Coastguard Service, which is run by the Maritime and Coastguard Agency (MCA). There are 18 maritime rescue centres or coastguard stations – see the list on the MCA site. Working weeks are typically 42 hours, involving 12-hour shifts. When jobs are advertised, it is either nationally and through the MCA website or locally through the operations centres/coastguard stations. Contact your local station if you are interested in applying for coastguard rescue officer volunteer work.

What It Pays

Starting salaries for coastguard watch assistants are around £12,500 per year, watch officers earn between £15,000 and £20,000 per year, with additional shift allowances (about 25 per cent of salary) and uniform provided.

Prospects

There are only 500 or so coastguard officers employed nationally, making this a relatively small profession. There are also around 3,000 voluntary auxiliary coastguards, assisting in this work. Promotion prospects exist, with higher level jobs available as station officer and district officer; these promotions require further qualifications and training.

Best Advice

Check out the MCA website for good information and recent press releases about coastguard activities.

Contacts

The Maritime and Coastguard Agency, Human Resources Recruitment Team, Bay 3/19 Spring Place, 105 Commercial Road, Southampton SO15 1EG
023 8032 308   www.mcga.gov.uk

Colourist/Colour Technician

Fashion, clothing and textile designers source fabrics from all over the world and need to be sure that a clothing or textile run is dyed to the same colour throughout, ensuring consistency for each and every garment or product. Colourists might be employed by the fibre/wool or yarn manufacturers to select dyes for different products, or they may provide mood boards, showing various shades of colour, from which designers can work.

The Job Description

Colourists actually source colours to match designers' requirements and work on trend prediction for each season's colours. They may work two to three years in advance to ensure that manufacturers produce cloth or textiles that will fit with a future trend. They have to be expert in forecasting future trends and assist trend prediction agencies and designers. They will choose the colour ranges for manufacturers' future products and may also be employed by large retail companies to verify that batches of products – whether they are sheets, towels or cardigans – have colour consistency throughout the batch.

The Person Specification

This is a job for someone who is passionate about colour and has the eye to notice tiny variations within a shade. Colourists need to be comfortable with the technical processes that produce different colours and able to distinguish the slightest difference of pigment. They also need to be interested in fashion, trends and textiles. You would need to be:

- creative, with a good eye for colour
- keen to keep up to date with trends, new textile processes and dyeing techniques
- interested in working in retail or for textile manufacturers
- able to make tough decisions – if a batch is wrong, there will be a big cost implication
- technically minded and innovative.

What It Takes

Some people will train as an apprentice dyeing technician, learning about the technical processes that go to making dyes and colours, with a textile manufacturer. You would need GCSEs or equivalent (D grade and over) in English, maths, science and perhaps art for entry to apprenticeships. Alternatively you could take a vocational route and study a BTEC or Diploma level course in textiles or even study for university level textile-related courses. Four GCSEs at C grade or equivalent, including English, maths, art and a science will be needed for BTEC National Diploma courses and a good GCSE profile, C grades and over, plus A levels/ Diploma will be needed for degree/Foundation degrees.

What Else

Outside the fashion and retail/textile industries, colourists may be used for a range of other products or processes in, for example, the automobile or interior design industries.

What It Pays

Starting salaries are in the range £12,000–£15,000 per year, but a colourist with experience and a great eye may be in great demand and therefore salaries could be considerably higher.

Prospects

Trend prediction agencies, fashion magazines and global textile manufacturers may be in need of colour consultation to ensure future profitability, so some colourists can work as consultants on a freelance basis.

Best Advice

Develop your colour/pigment awareness. Take textiles courses at school or college. Try and get some work experience with an interior design or textile company. Work hard at sciences – particularly chemistry.

Contacts

The Society of Dyers and Colourists, PO Box 244, 82 Grattan Road, Bradford BD1 2JB
01274 725138   www.sdc.org.uk

Skillfast-UK
www.skillfast-uk.org

Comedy Writer

This may seem like quite a wacky idea – especially if you are keen to write jokes or sketches for comedy shows or comedians. In essence though, it is much like any other kind of writing. If you have the talent to write in a funny way that makes other people laugh, then you will need determination and motivation to make this your career. You will also need to have a thick skin in order to deal with rejection.

The Job Description

This job can take many forms, from writing one-off jokes, stories or gags to whole sketches or shows. While, in a sense, this ability to write for comedy might be a natural talent, to make a living from this requires considerable dedication, practice and honing of your writing skills. It is more than likely that you will be working freelance or contract-to-contract for TV companies or individuals who need to make use of your talent. Typically, you will use your observation skills to come up with offbeat ideas, which you can turn into script ideas, actual scripts or sketches or one-off jokes that you will then have to sell to your potential clients. So often the smallest part of the job is the idea generation and writing, with more time being spent on the 'pitch': how and when and to whom you try to sell your work.

The Person Specification

Writers often say that whether they get paid for it or not, to them writing is like breathing. They don't necessarily plan to do it, it's just that in their head, words and phrases are linking up together constantly, and in their life they notice things in different ways, which for comedy writers becomes their comic take on life. So you'll probably know if this is you. Being the funny kid in the playground might be an indication of talent, but you'll also need to be:

- almost obsessed with writing comedy, jokes, gags, etc.
- creative, possibly not entirely Joe/Jane Normal – that's to say that you will see/hear/feel things with a different, perhaps comic slant
- good with words and aware of comic nuances
- confident about promoting your ideas to anyone and everyone
- determined and thorough in researching possible buyers of your work
- able to take constant rejection
- flexible enough to rewrite and make adaptations to your writing.

What It Takes

There's no sure-fire way to get into comedy writing, but some things might help. There are obvious things like working hard at English, researching other comedy writers and developing a unique style. University courses in creative writing might help, but in general comedy writers have lived a bit and use material from this life experience in their writing. Sometimes a miserable experience is turned into great material for writing, so comedy writers use everything. You may find it useful to travel a bit, study at university, work in something else that interests you (known as 'the day job') while you develop your talent. Many comedy writers get involved in productions at university (think Cambridge Footlights) and try out ideas for the future.

There are one-day comedy writing workshops that can be extremely useful – Planet Comedy offers these in topics such as stand-up comedy, sketch and sitcom writing. They cover formula gag writing, sketch construction, script layout, pitch writing, contacting the right people, etc.

The National Academy of Writing also offers events, workshops and courses on writing.

What Else

The tried and tested formula of bombarding producers/directors of TV/radio companies with examples of your work is still a common way of letting the right people know what you can do. Contacting the agents of comedians that you would like to write for would be another possible route to work.

The BBC Talent scheme is one way of trying to get yourself discovered, though there is intense competition for places.

What It Pays

This is a pretty impossible one to gauge, but a TV company that requested films or comedy sketches from students was offering £250 per filmed sketch and £100 per written piece, but if you make a reputation for yourself, you will earn way in excess of those rates.

Prospects

Some comic writers move into the film industry, so Hollywood might be your next destination.

Best Advice

Keep writing and trying out work on friends to gauge their reaction. Analyse the work of comedy writers you like. Keep observing everything that you see around you. Make contact with anyone who could act as a mentor to you.

Contacts

National Academy of Writing, University of Central England, Margaret Street, Birmingham B3 3BX
0121 331 5963   www.thenationalacademyofwriting.org.uk

Planet Comedy, Fit2Fill
www.planetcomedy.co.uk

BBC Talent
www.bbc.co.uk/talent

Community Support Worker (CSW)/ Social Care Assistant

CSWs work with a range of people who might need support and encouragement. They may support adults with mental health problems/ learning disabilities who need help to be independent. They might work where their clients, often called service users, live (which might be in a community home, for example, or sheltered accommodation), or they might visit them regularly to check up on them and offer them support and encouragement. Service users could be schizophrenic or depressed or they might have a condition such as Down's syndrome.

CSWs can work caring for anyone who is being supported by social services or a charity. Sometimes, as a community/family support worker, they may work in a family support centre, offering hands-on help to children, young people and families. Increasingly CSWs are being re-named 'social care assistants', and there is currently a recruitment drive to encourage people into this profession. If you did this job you would be working alongside social workers and health professionals; your role would be essentially practical and supportive in helping people live ordinary lives, encouraging independence and resourcefulness in people who may be disadvantaged, disabled or have personal problems.

The Job Description
CSWs will support clients in a number of ways, including taking them shopping, going to appointments with them, helping them with their own basic personal care and cooking basic meals. They might help a client gain confidence in taking a bus into town or using a local launderette. They will also arrange fun activities and outings for service users and their families, even organising holidays.

The Person Specification
Support workers are committed to helping their clients achieve independence, and they do this by building up a client's confidence through encouragement and support. They have to be non-judgemental and caring, sensitive to a client's feelings and fears and be able to think and act calmly. For this work, you would need to be:

- caring and interested in helping people with mental health/disabilities
- practical, energetic and levelheaded
- a problem solver
- sensitive and empathetic
- patient and tolerant
- a good communicator.

What It Takes

There are no specific entry qualifications, as a range of qualifications and/or experience is accepted. Often vocational intermediate or A level/ Diploma level qualifications in health and social care or subjects like sociology and psychology can be useful. For childcare-related roles, the BTEC in Childhood Studies or NVQs in Childcare/Care are often relevant. Voluntary experience in care would be a valuable way to see if you have what it takes for this work.

What Else

Some aspects of this care work can involve the bathing and washing of clients and taking responsibility for medication.

What It Pays

Typical pay rates are around the £13,000–£16,000 per year range.

Prospects

You could move into social work or learning disability nursing from this work.

Best Advice

Try and gain volunteer experience to see how you find this caring role. Community Service Volunteers offer placements across the UK in support work.

Contacts

General Social Care Council, Goldings House, 2 Hay's Lane, London SE1 2HB
020 7397 5800   www.gscc.org.uk

Social Care and Social Work Careers Information website
www.socialworkcareers.co.uk

Community Service Volunteers
www.csv.org.uk

Compost Guru/
Environmental Education Officer

This is going to sound like a mad career idea but, in fact, given the limited resources on the planet, the reasons for recycling and good environmental practices are becoming pretty compelling. Environmental education work can nonetheless seem rather dull and worthy, so local authorities and organisations who wish to promote positive environmental practices sometimes advertise the work of environmental education officers as compost guru-ing.

To start with, environmental education work is not just about advising on compost; officers, or gurus, work for central/local government and environmental charities/pressure groups, and their mission is to raise awareness of the environment and the need to conserve and preserve what exists by teaching good recycling and conservation practices to communities and individuals.

The Job Description
Education officers can get involved in projects with schools and communities dedicated to preserving wildlife environments, work at environmental education centres, or give advice to companies on sound waste practices and encourage a more thoughtful awareness of the environmental impact of developments in a local area. They offer training in home composting and waste minimisation. They encourage more 'green' awareness through events and promotions. Newly appointed compost gurus set up training schemes for local residents to encourage composting initiatives. Sometimes they recruit willing volunteers and train them as volunteer compost gurus with the task of influencing their local neighbourhood.

The Person Specification
The range of activities within this job role can be extremely diverse; officers/gurus have to be multi-skilled, with the technical experience to give advice and offer consultancy to individuals, community groups or organisations. For this work you will need to be:

- committed to environmental conservation
- prepared to do a hands-on conservation job and/or manage a project and a team of workers
- prepared to give talks to local people and schools
- capable of offering consultancy on environmental developments and the impact of building/planning initiatives
- prepared to become an expert on recycling and composting.

What It Takes

To succeed at this job you will need scientific/technical skills related to conservation and the environment, as well as the people skills to persuade and inform people of threats to the environment. Most people take agricultural/horticultural/environmental science/conservation/ecology degrees to gain expertise in these areas. You will need five GCSEs with C grade and over, or equivalent, and 2–3 A levels or a Diploma, or equivalent, featuring science- and/or geography-based subjects, to gain a place on environmentally focused university courses. There may also be Foundation degrees in related subjects, for which entry requirements may be lower than ordinary degrees.

Most people also need experience in community environmental volunteering, either as a voluntary countryside ranger, or with the British Trust for Conservation Volunteers, to get the practical skills needed.

What Else

Many environment-based projects are government short-term or contract-to-contract initiatives that do not offer reliable job progression. Nonetheless, experience on these kinds of projects or initiatives is considered vital for a career in environmental education.

What It Pays

Starting salaries are around £17,000–£18,500 per year.

Prospects

There may be possibilities for work abroad once you have gained experience – see VSO www.vso.org.uk.

Best Advice

Work with BTCV (British Trust for Conservation Volunteers) or Groundwork as a volunteer to gain the practical skills you need.

Contacts

The Institute of Ecology and Environmental Management, 45 Southgate Street, Winchester, Hants SO23 9EH
01962 868626   www.ieem.net

Countryside Jobs Service
www.countryside-jobs.com

Groundwork
www.groundwork.org.uk

BTCV
www.btcv.org

Computer Games Tester

Playing computer games for a living – if you're wondering whether anyone really gets to do that and earn money at the same time, then the answer is yes. Computer games testers assess how games work and how challenging particular games can be. So if you're a passionate or even obsessive computer games player, then this job might be for you. Testers have to check the quality of games from the initial 'build' stage to the final prototype, which has to be tested at every level, so that bugs are identified. Games may take months or even years to be developed; obviously you would have to be an expert game player yourself to do this work, otherwise you wouldn't last long enough in some of the more complex games to check the highest proficiency levels.

The Job Description

Testers or quality assurance (QA) testers are vital in the games industry in order to check that some seemingly wonderful game created by a programmer actually works without errors or glitches. Most of the errors are technical problems, not anticipated by designers, to do with art or graphics work, sound, level of difficulty, points accumulation or even areas of plot confusion. Testers have to scrutinise each area of a game methodically and relentlessly, at all potential levels, and write reports describing each problem, making suggestions. Unless a tester has uncovered every potential problem, they are just playing at the job.

The Person Specification

It is essential that games testers detect program defects in pre-release versions of games while assessing their playability, so they need to be expert game players with extraordinary manual dexterity. In addition, they need to be:

- well organised
- able to write detailed reports
- computer literate
- passionate about game playing
- determined and committed to uncovering problems.

What It Takes

Not surprisingly, a high level of expertise at computer games can actually be all it takes to get into this work as that is the most essential skill needed. Computer games companies seem to expect a minimum of GCSE maths and English (or equivalent) and that applicants should be passionate and expert games players. You would also need to be:

- able to play games for extended periods of time

- in possession, ideally, of technical computer skills and familiar with programming.

It might be useful, therefore, to take vocational information technology qualifications at college, such as Diplomas or A levels in applied subjects, before applying for jobs. Another way of training could be through Skillset, which is launching a new apprenticeship in Quality Assurance (QA) testing; details can be found on their website. There are also Foundation and Practitioner Certificates in Software Testing for people working in the industry to gain accreditation and develop their skills; this is available through the Information Systems Exam Board (ISEB) – see website.

What Else

An understanding of the programming and design side of the industry can be useful, so some people take foundation degree or degree courses in software development/computer programming, interactive media, multimedia design or even computer games design.

It's worth keeping up to date with industry news through specialist magazines for the computer or electronic entertainment industry, and, of course, get plenty of experience of game playing across a range of games.

What It Pays

Starting pay for new entrants is around £10,000–£15,000 per year.

Prospects

With experience it may be possible to move into work as a producer. Producers coordinate the testing and keep the development of a game on schedule and to budget. Companies also employ games counsellors who field questions from players over the phone or by email and give hints and tips on how to win, and this might be an alternative area of work for games testers.

Best Advice

Become an expert at playing computer games and study ICT at school. Read the specialist magazines and check websites for computer games companies like Eidos, who produce good careers information on opportunities for gamers in the computer industry. Visit the London Games Career Fair, where all the leading companies are represented – www.gamecareerfair.com.

Contacts

Eidos Interactive UK (one of the biggest UK computer games manufacturers), Wimbledon Bridge House, 1 Hartfield Road, Wimbledon, London SW19 3RU
020 8636 3000   www.eidos.co.uk

International Games Development Assocation (IGDA)
www.igda.org/breakingin

Blitz Games
www.blitzgames.com

Codemasters
www.codemasters.co.uk

Skillset
www.skillset.org/careers

ISEB
www.iseb.org.uk

Games Tester
www.gamestester.com

Countryside Manager/ Ranger/Warden

If you're the kind of person who hates the idea of an indoor job, then this kind of work might seem right for you. Ranger work is about protecting the environment and allowing the general public access to wild and natural areas. Countryside management is the general term for this kind of work and there are many different job types within this category. Essentially, there are managers who run national and local nature reserves, country parks and recreation areas whose work includes managing a team of rangers or wardens, planning work and controlling budgets. Then there are rangers or wardens who have a more hands-on role in practical conservation activities in the countryside, perhaps including surveys of species, scrub management, hedge laying, pond digging, stone wall construction or educational work with children and other visitors.

The Job Description

Managers might be responsible for a conservation area, forests, rivers or farms. Their work might involve wildlife protection, species or habitat management, as well as visitor attractions, tourism and ecological or environmental education initiatives. Rangers or wardens can be involved in tree surveys and re-planting, landscaping work, wildlife tours, restoration work and practical environmental work for regeneration purposes. They often have to act in an educational role for school parties and visitors.

The Person Specification

If you are interested in being a ranger, then you would need to be:

- keen to work outdoors in natural, wild or even remote locations
- interested in the national environment
- practical and resourceful
- committed to conservation
- prepared to work in unpleasant weather conditions.

In addition, for more specialised ranger or warden work, skills in habitat management, wildlife and species field surveys and a fascination with plants and animals may be required. At manager level, additional business and management skills to ensure the financial viability of projects and research, as well as team leadership skills, will be needed. An almost scientific approach to conservation issues and an understanding of eco-tourism are also necessary for anyone working in this career area.

What It Takes

More and more people who go into this work, even at the more practical ranger level, have degree-level qualifications in environmental conservation subjects. Many graduates take on a ranger's job at the beginning of their careers to gain on-the-ground experience and then move onto management or field research posts. Remember that this can be quite a scientific, even technical job.

There are college level (below degree standard) courses in conservation, gamekeeping or forestry which may also lead into ranger work, but most people have to have substantial hands-on experience, often through volunteer work, to get a start in this area. There are also foundation degrees in forestry and conservation/ecology which would be useful for this work.

For management, research, or countryside site management, a relevant ecological or environmental degree is probably essential.

What Else

This is an appealing and popular type of work and there is strong competition for jobs. To gain a first post in this kind of work at ranger or manager level, voluntary work and experience in a range of settings is almost essential. Try out vacation work experience with the British Conservation Trust for Volunteers (BCTV) or with voluntary ranger services throughout the UK. The Royal Society for the Protection of Birds (RSPB) also has a voluntary bird warden scheme, which would be valuable experience.

What It Pays

Pay rates vary across the country and according to employers, but pay for rangers could start at £16,000–£20,000 per year.

Prospects

The Countryside Management Association lists about 530,000 members but many of these will be volunteer or student members. As many of these jobs are for charities or in the government sector, there will also be limits on number of jobs and pay scales. There are nonetheless roughly 1,300 local/county or borough councils employing countryside staff, and interest in conservation of natural resources is a growth area.

The major employers are national agencies like Natural England, the National Trust and the Environment Agency, national and regional parks authorities, local councils and charities like the RSPB. Competition can be intense for permanent vacancies, but there are often short-term or seasonal contracts for rangers in the busy summer period.

Best Advice

Do some volunteering, preferably with some skills-based work and accreditation such as the BCTV courses. Research the most suitable college or university-level courses available to you. Get the broadest range of experience possible with a variety of agencies or charities, whether this is paid or voluntary.

Contacts

The Countryside Management Association, Writtle College, Lordship Road, Writtle, Chelmsford, Essex LM1 3RR
01245 424116   www.countrysidemanagement.org.uk

Natural England
www.naturalengland.org.uk

British Conservation Trust for Volunteers
www.bctv.org.uk

Contact the BCTV for details of voluntary work and courses in rural skills and crafts, which will be valuable for your future employment. Also contact your local area council or Countryside Ranger Service about any volunteer ranger service that may be operating in your area.

The Countryside Jobs Service produces a job vacancy bulletin which gives an excellent range of countryside jobs across the UK.
www.countryside-jobs.com

Court Reporter/Verbatim Reporter

You may have seen a court reporter in a TV programme or film, using a machine to take detailed transcripts of court proceedings, which may have to be read back to a judge. Court reporters are responsible for recording a word-for-word account of evidence, judgments and speeches in court proceedings.

The Job Description

Court reporters (also known as shorthand writers) attend court sessions and make shorthand records using a stenotype machine or by hand. They use a computer-aided transcription (CAT) system, to create a verbatim transcription, which may be edited at the end of the day. As a general rule, the judge might check this record to determine its accuracy as a true record of what was said. While court work is the most well-known type of verbatim reporting, reporters can also be employed by other public organisations that require a detailed transcript of proceedings. Increasingly verbatim reporters are being required to produce 'real time' records of exchanges in court or public settings. This means that what is being said is produced virtually instantly on a big screen, directly from the stenotype machine. In addition there are some reporters who are also qualified to take notes for deaf and hearing-impaired people in courts and other situations by converting any speech to text (STT).

The Person Specification

Reporters need excellent English, good concentration and attention to detail. It helps if they are interested in law and current affairs. Sometimes the speech of witnesses has to be rendered clearly comprehensible, without changing the actual meaning, and this requires accuracy and skill. The key skills of the reporter are speed and accuracy, with shorthand speeds of at least 180 words per minute expected, with 200 words per minute for 'real time' recording. They have to be ready to read back aloud in court what has been said, on request, and transcribe a day's proceedings in the evening, if lawyers require it. You will need to be:

- a good communicator, especially with excellent listening skills
- able to pay attention to detail
- extremely careful about grammar and spelling
- capable of using specialist software
- accurate and set yourself high standards
- prepared to work long and irregular hours
- ready to train in typing, pen and machine shorthand and practise regularly to retain your speed of transcription.

What It Takes
Most reporters take specialised courses in machine shorthand through a college or by distance learning. These courses are recommended by the British Institute of Verbatim Reporters. New trainees normally take a further 3–12 months to increase their speeds. Most courses require four GCSE passes or equivalent, including English.

What Else
Reporters may also be employed in the House of Commons and House of Lords. To be an accredited STTR (Speech to Text Reporter) it is worth checking the CACDP (Council for the Advancement of Communication with Deaf People) website which has information about the work and a directory which lists reporters.

What It Pays
Verbatim or court reporters are generally paid in the region of £15,000–£20,000 per year.

Prospects
The BBC and other organisations also use transcribers for subtitles for television and media.

Best Advice
Develop manual dexterity and excellent English skills.

Contacts
Her Majesty's Courts Service, Clive House, Petty France, London SW1H 9HD
020 7189 2000   www.hmcourts-service.gov.uk

The British Institute of Verbatim Reporters
www.bivr.org.uk

CACDP
www.cacdp.org.uk

Crime Scene Investigator (CSI)/Scenes of Crime Officer (SOCO)

Crime scene investigators/scenes of crime officers (often referred to as SOCOs) are responsible for assisting criminal investigations by recording, recovering and collating forensic evidence from crime and incident scenes. This involves painstaking searches for evidence, taking photographs of crime scenes and exhibits, and the recording of evidence on computer databases.

The Job Description

Crime scene evidence can be easily contaminated, so attention to detail and strict procedures are vital for this work. Being able to notice, assess and record exactly what needs to be analysed is also crucial. Typically a CSI will be called out to the scene of the crime as part of a team, which will undertake to uncover and recover every piece of vital evidence pertinent to the case. This may be for a burglary or car break-in, or for something more serious. They take charge of the scene, taking photos, fingerprints or footprints, checking for carpet fibres and collecting samples of blood or hair. The rest of their time is spent in transporting or protecting evidence, recording it using computers, or in the laboratory transferring evidence for safe keeping. They might also have to produce a written record of the details of the evidence gathered.

The Person Specification

This is not a job for the squeamish, and is far less glamorous than TV or films might suggest. It is much more likely to involve painstaking attention to detail and rigorous protection of a crime scene. You would need to be objective, detached and highly analytical. You would be responsible for collecting the evidence that builds a case – nothing could be missed or overlooked. Certainly an eye for often microscopic detail is valued for this work. You would need to be:

- scientific/technical in the way you approach things
- experienced in dealing with difficult or traumatic situations
- self-motivated and able to work on your own initiative
- a good communicator for face-to-face work and for report writing of your findings
- good at working in a police team
- interested in the investigation of crime.

What It Takes

There are two main job roles offered in crime scene investigation. For assistant crime scene investigator, GCSE passes, at C grade and over, or equivalent, in a range of subjects including maths, English and science plus preferably A levels/Diploma or equivalent in sciences are required. For crime scene investigator, most applicants have degrees in biology or chemistry or similar, or possibly a forensic science degree. It seems that, due to the popularity of this work, applicants with higher than the minimum qualifications are more often than not recruited to this work.

Training takes place on the job and through training courses at the NPIA (National Police Improvement Agency) centre in County Durham. Initial training may take about nine weeks, with further courses every year to update and extend training. Once fully trained and qualified for five years, it is possible to move on to the Durham University Crime Scene Diploma.

There are some interesting developments in courses and training. In conjunction with the NPIA, the University of Teesside is offering a Foundation degree in Fingerprint Identification which is the only recognised university qualification for fingerprint officer work. This university also has a crime scene science degree course.

What Else

It is possible to pay privately for the NPIA course (£9,000 approximately) and then apply for CSI work.

What It Pays

Starting salaries are around £18,000–£26,000 per year.

Prospects

Jobs advertised in this type of work attract large numbers of applicants and are mainly advertised with constabularies – see www.policecouldyou.co.uk. As there will be lots of applicants for every vacancy, you should make sure you have the best skills and experience in order to showcase yourself in your applications. Once trained and qualified, job opportunities are available throughout the UK and overseas.

Best Advice

Gain any experience you can with the police. Many constabularies offer voluntary experience through specific schemes or by request. Study hard at sciences and perhaps consider specific university courses that offer hands-on experience with crime scenes.

Contacts

The NPIA Centre, Harperley Hall, Crook, County Durham DL15 8DS
01368 762191   www.npia.police.uk

Criminal Psychologist/Profiler

These two jobs are related, and in some cases profiling work is an extension of criminal psychology (often referred to as forensic psychology). Criminal/forensic psychologists work mainly in prisons and detention centres with offenders, helping them to come to terms with their antisocial or offending behaviour through one-to-one therapy or group sessions. Profilers assist the police in assembling a profile of an unknown offender, who they might be keen to interview regarding a crime that has been committed.

The Job Description

Psychologists working in prisons or with offenders are trained to analyse behaviour so that they can identify abnormal patterns of thinking, which can then be addressed through counselling or therapy. They are also responsible for risk assessment of offenders and recommendations for possible treatment. They will probably decide on the best treatment programme likely to help rehabilitate an offender. On the investigative side, they can help the police in crime detection and offender profiling. They work in prisons, young offenders' institutions, secure hospitals for the National Health Service, in treatment centres and for the police force. They may also act as experts in court cases and advise on sentencing.

The Person Specification

This work could be quite troubling, unless you are able to be non-judgemental and objective about your clients. For most people, the idea of helping rapists or sex offenders talk about their behaviour would not be appealing. You would need to be intrigued by the reasons for criminal behaviour and committed to preventing it. You would need to:

- be able to develop a relationship with offenders
- understand the science and sociology of behaviour
- be interested in helping people make changes to their behaviour and even predict future behaviour
- be able to manage statistical information and make sense of it
- develop evaluation techniques to assess the behaviour of prisoners
- be well organised, computer literate and able to work well with other crime professionals
- tolerate a certain amount of risk, because of time spent amongst people within the criminal justice system
- be confident about making decisions on the release of offenders back into the community.

What It Takes

It takes a long time to be skilled and experienced in this field, so you will need to be highly motivated. Your first step will be to gain five GCSE passes (C grade and above) or equivalent, including English, maths and science, followed by two to three A levels/Diploma or equivalent. Many students take A levels in law and psychology as a way of checking their interest in this career, although this is not essential.

You will then need to study a British Psychological Society (BPS) accredited degree in psychology – most have a criminal psychology component. To complete this training, most psychology graduates apply for the highly sought-after psychological assistant jobs that become available with HM Prison Service Psychological Services, and complete a two-year Master's qualification in forensic psychology in parallel with a work contract. As you can imagine, there is intense competition for these training jobs as a psychological assistant. Other applicants may choose to study clinical psychology in a hospital setting and move into the forensic/criminal side after experience and further study.

What Else
Forensic/criminal psychology

There are about 139 prisons in England and Wales and therefore forensic psychology posts might be available within these institutions and those of the Scottish Prison Service. Psychologists may be brought in by the police to work on specific cases or even to become involved in areas such as hostage negotiation.

Criminal profiler

The work of a criminal profiler may be a future career move for a forensic/criminal psychologist but be aware that job opportunities in profiling work are extremely few and far between. This is because profiling is often a job undertaken by a range of other professionals such as police, clinical psychologists or therapists and current figures for employed criminal profilers suggest that there may be as few as 29 people employed overall in the UK in a specifically profiling role.

What It Pays

Starting salary for a prison psychologist is in the range of £16,468–£19,290 per year. Psychological assistants can be paid from £10,000–£16,000 per year.

Prospects

There are further opportunities in crime research through university departments and the Home Office Crime Research Unit.

Best Advice

Work hard at maths, English and sciences and gain the highest grades possible at GCSE or equivalent and A level/Diploma or equivalent. While studying at university, try some volunteering with your local Youth Offending Team (part of Social Services) or as a prison visitor – contact your local prison. Research the criminal justice system.

Contacts

British Psychological Society, St Andrews House, 48 Princess Road East, Leicester LE1 7DR
0116 254 9568   www.bps.org.uk

HM Prison Service
www.hmprisonservice.gov.uk

National Probation Service
www.probation.homeoffice.gov.uk

Croupier

Croupiers, or dealers, work in casinos and are in direct contact with club members or visitors, assisting in the various games that are available – from roulette to blackjack. There are over 140 casinos in the UK listed on the British Casinos Association website, operating under strict legal controls and licensing arrangements, which make it a very specialised business.

The Job Description

Dealers or croupiers have to be confident in dealing with customers, skilled at understanding the rules of the game and be able to project themselves in a calm, competent manner. Croupiers will manage the game at their table, working on the casino floor, checking chips, explaining rules and calculating payouts. The most popular gaming tables are roulette, blackjack and poker. Each dealer must have a detailed knowledge of the games that he/she oversees. Their responsibility is to manage their game in such a way that customers enjoy themselves and the casino earns money from customers coming back to play again. Customer service and money handling are key aspects of the role. Standards of dress are high and most casinos provide appropriate attire for their staff.

The Person Specification

It takes about 6–8 weeks to learn the skills and techniques required to become a dealer or croupier and you would need:

- an aptitude for quick mental calculations
- good manual dexterity
- a self-confident, outgoing manner
- good concentration
- excellent customer service skills, including being able to be tactful when required.

You would also need to be over 18 years of age and pass Criminal Records Bureau (CRB) clearance to prove you have no criminal convictions.

What It Takes

Casinos train staff so that they are confident to do the job correctly. Training is through on-the-job paid experience with supervision or through short courses of 6–8 weeks. Successful applicants are generally expected to have GCSE or equivalent passes in English and maths. The newly formed Regional Gaming Academy at Blackpool College offers a range of courses in casino operations with a Foundation degree in Casino Operations Management, and the University of Salford offers a Gambling and Leisure Management degree course; both would be useful ways to gain experience and skills for management careers in the gaming industry.

What Else
Unsocial hours are an essential part of this work, so be prepared to work late evenings, early mornings and weekends with typical shifts being from 2 to 10p.m. or 10p.m. to 6a.m. The job can be physically and mentally tiring.

What It Pays
Starting salaries can be around £11,500–£18,500 per year.

Prospects
The starting point for careers in the casino business is always at croupier/ dealer level, but promotion can lead to management or training roles. With two years' experience you could apply for work on cruise ships, while Las Vegas or Monte Carlo might be a possibility with substantial experience. For these prestigious jobs you would be expected to impress at a dealer audition as part of the selection process.

Best Advice
This may be the kind of work to try out on a temporary or part-time basis to find out if it suits you. Try to contact a local casino to arrange a visit – the British Casino Association's website lists the main casinos in the UK and recruitment contacts at each casino.

Contacts
The British Casino Association, 38 Grosvenor Gardens, London SW1 0EB
020 7730 1055   www.britishcasinoassociation.org.uk

Regional Gaming Academy, Blackpool and the Fylde College
www.blackpool.ac.uk

Gambling Commission
www.gamblingcommission.gov.uk

Dance Teacher/Instructor

There are many ways to become a dance teacher and it is often a second career for professional dancers who want to pass their skills and experience on. People choose to learn to dance for many reasons – they may hope to have a career as a performer, or because they want to dance for a hobby/interest, or for fitness. As a teacher, you have to understand the individual dance motivation of each student. While the instruction part of the job will involve you explaining how to learn dance techniques, you will also have to be able to demonstrate them.

The Job Description

Dance teachers aim to encourage their students to develop skills in different dance styles, normally including jazz and ballet. You could be working in a school, college, gym or dance studio with young students or adults. For those of your students wishing to go on to performance, you will offer training in graded ballet exams and possibly jazz, tap and modern dancing. In mainstream schools and colleges you might be teaching dance as a means of artistic expression or as another way to encourage physical fitness. In gyms or studios, the work can be a mixture of performance- and fitness-based classes.

The Person Specification

Most dance teachers have reached a high standard in dance themselves, either through graded exams followed by dance or ballet school training, or through specialist degree courses in dance theatre or contemporary dance. You will need to have a high standard of practical ability in dance and performance and be prepared to work with individuals or groups. In schools, you will probably teach dance within the drama curriculum or alongside another school subject. You will need to be:

- patient with good communication skills
- enthusiastic about dance
- able to encourage others in the development of dance skills
- able to control and motivate a class group
- aware of the stresses of dance exercise on the body and how to prevent strains
- able to promote dance as an exercise for all ages and abilities.

What It Takes

At the lowest level, most dance teachers or instructors in private schools or gyms will have Royal Academy of Dance (RAD) or equivalent graded exam qualifications plus a dance teaching certificate or gym instructor certificate, such as that offered by the YMCA. The YMCA provides a wide range of courses that offer dance instructor training for work in gyms and health clubs and these would be sufficient for most adult classes.

For work in mainstream schools or colleges, you would need higher level qualifications such as a dance and/or drama degree followed by a teaching qualification. The teaching qualification needed to give you Qualified Teacher Status (QTS) is called a Postgraduate Certificate of Education (PGCE). The Royal Academy of Dance offers a specialist PGCE in Dance Teaching which could be studied after a relevant dance degree. In general, schools are keen to recruit applicants who can teach in more than one subject area, for example dance and drama.

What Else

It's worth thinking whether you have the enthusiasm to teach someone who struggles to be coordinated or has very little natural talent.

You can only teach someone to pass the exam boards for dance exams by being an accredited instructor through, for example, the RAD. The Council for Dance Education and Training (CDET) lists accredited dance teachers in a directory on their site.

What It Pays

This is variable according to the type of work you do. Primary and secondary school work will pay in the region of £21,000 upwards. Private schools may only pay you an hourly rate and this will involve evening and weekend work.

Prospects

Demand for dance teachers is high at present, but it is also possible to move into areas such as dance therapy and choreography if you have a degree (or equivalent) qualification in dance.

Best Advice

You need to develop your own talent as much as possible by practising and gaining accredited qualifications through one of the main dance exam boards (RAD) and through performance and dance college/university courses.

Contacts

Council for Dance Education and Training (CDET), Old Brewer's Yard, 17–19 Neal Street, Covent Garden, London WC2H 9UY
020 7240 5703   www.cdet.org.uk

Royal Academy of Dance
www.rad.org.uk

Deaf Signer/Lip-reader/Lip-speaker

These three jobs have a common purpose in helping and supporting deaf people, or those with a hearing impairment, by communicating with them in a way that is acceptable and most suitable for them.

Deaf signing is used as the preferred communication tool by deaf people, and is needed as a skill by nurses, social workers, deaf students and anybody working within the deaf or hearing-impaired community.

Lip-reading is a technique that can be taught to deaf people or those who are beginning to lose their hearing (or even nosey people who like to listen in to conversations at a distance) as a way of helping them to understand and make the most of the world around them.

Lip-speaking is a silent method of speaking with clear mouth movements; lip-readers are then able to read what is being said from these mouth movements.

All these skills can be immensely valuable for deaf and hearing-impaired people.

The Job Description

Some people use these skills as part of their job, but there is a demand for people who can use these skills for TV work, conferences, for educational support in colleges or universities, for legal and court work and in business.

Jobs for deaf signers are found through agencies or as one-off support contracts for deaf people – for doctor's appointments, for interviews with a bank manager, during the delivery of a baby, for solicitor's meetings, for events or conferences and for certain TV programmes. Some holiday companies consider deaf signing as important as having a foreign language when recruiting resort staff.

As around 50,000 people in the UK use sign language (British Sign Language, BSL) as their first language, it is an incredibly powerful communication tool.

Jobs for lip-reading teachers, who often have experience of working within the deaf community and may also use BSL, exist at colleges and community centres. Being able to help people whose hearing is failing stay in communication with those around them by teaching them lip-reading can be very rewarding.

At conferences/events and in university lectures or on TV programmes, it is becoming common to offer a lip-speaker to interpret what is being said by a hearing speaker to non-hearing audience members.

The Person Specification

People who do this work are committed to an inclusive society where everyone has a 'voice'. Many people who do this work have experienced, through their work or family, the challenges faced by deaf or hearing-impaired people in their lives. You would need to be:

- prepared to learn and practise BSL sign language or lip-speaking
- aware of courtesy issues with deaf people, such as facing them when you sign or lip-speak, standing in good light and avoiding covering your mouth
- willing to understand the deaf as people who belong to a different cultural group, rather than just as people with a disability
- ready to ask the deaf and hearing impaired how they would prefer to communicate.

What It Takes

There are many and varied courses in signing, lip-reading and lip-speaking recommended by the Council for the Advancement of Communication with Deaf People (CACDP), including BSL courses at Levels 1, 2 and 3. To be an interpreter, you will need to achieve the NVQ Level 4 qualification in interpreting as well. Check your local colleges and the CACDP website. There are some university courses which offer interpreting qualifications – these are listed on the CACDP website.

What Else

Job vacancies exist in interpreting and sign language tutoring throughout the UK. This is a valuable extra to show on your CV, but, as with any language, you have to keep your skill up to speed through practice.

What It Pays

Pay rates for qualified sign language interpreters can be between £20,000 and £30,000 per year, but there are also agencies that recruit people for one-off work. Hourly rates can be between £20 and £30 per hour.

Prospects

These skills can be used in a number of careers, including the education and social care sectors, in youth work, TV, theatre, business and conferencing.

Best Advice

Start now on BSL Level 1 and 2 courses which are offered by many colleges through evening study for just a few hours per week. Do some volunteering in the deaf community and see how useful you will find these skills.

Contacts

Council for the Advancement of Communication with Deaf People, Durham University Science Park, Block 4, Stockton Road, Durham DH1 3HZ
0191 383 1155   Textphone: 0191 383 7915   www.cacdp.org.co.uk

Association of Sign Language Interpreters (ASLI)
www.asli.org.uk

Diver

Many people enjoy diving or snorkelling for pleasure, but the work of a commercial diver, though using the same techniques, is quite different and possibly less exciting. The range of work can vary from working offshore on an oil or gas field, to surveying wrecks or checking out harbour damage. Divers have to work in extremely arduous conditions and have to be highly disciplined, due to health and safety restrictions. In particular it is worth realising that, because the place of work is underwater, diving is simply the travel-to-work method.

The Job Description

Commercial divers are employed to check anything below sea or water level, including oil rigs or platforms, sewage pipes or ships' hulls. It is rarely about diving for treasure; in most situations, it is much more mundane than that and could involve sawing through steel girders (which might take hours below the surface) or pouring concrete.

A great deal of a commercial diver's work will be with the major gas and oil companies, generally called offshore commercial diving, and involves the laying and maintaining of pipes, digging trenches on the sea bed and general construction and maintenance work on oil rigs.

Inshore commercial divers might be diving in rivers, lakes, canals, etc. They can be involved in port or harbour reconstruction and repair; they may have to check propeller damage on a ship or use explosives to remove an obstruction. They may be doing surveying work for a civil engineering company or using welding techniques underwater.

Police divers are working police officers who have undertaken specialist training.

Whatever type of diving career you go for, there are strict health and safety guidelines which are set out by the Health and Safety Executive (HSE).

The Person Specification

Divers have to be able to put up with physical discomfort, and they have to be prepared to work in the dark and be cold and wet most of the time. Apparently a sense of humour helps, when having to deal with sewage, for example, and team work and self-discipline are vital. You would need to be:

- committed to being physically fit
- able to stay calm and act decisively when necessary
- keen to be in the water, and good at swimming and possibly snorkelling
- flexible and prepared to work unsocial hours (typically 8–10-hour days)

- aware of health and safety rules and the dangers that are part of the job, both for you and those you accompany.

What It Takes

The HSE website lists training centres which it approves and accredits to train commercial offshore and inland divers in the UK. Courses cover a range of aspects of commercial diving competence and may include diving medicine, elementary seamanship, small boat handling, use of diving equipment and the operation of hand tools.

Trainee divers have to pass a thorough medical exam before going for training, and professional divers have to undergo a medical assessment every year of their career.

If you are interested in civil and coastal engineering as well as diving, the University of Plymouth has a unique degree course which offers the chance of a chartered engineering qualification and an HSE diving qualification – see www.plymouth.ac.uk.

What Else

Many divers work on short-term contracts for contractors, and both inshore and offshore divers have to be prepared to travel anywhere in the world for work. Most divers only work 200 days per year.

What It Pays

Pay is at a daily rate and can be £60–£150 per day for inshore divers and between £120 and £1,000 per day for offshore divers. The pay rates reflect the danger levels of this career.

Prospects

Experienced divers can be promoted to diving supervisors, in charge of a team of divers, or they can take further courses to be underwater inspectors, who are trained to carry out underwater visual inspections.

Best Advice

Start by enjoying some recreational diving. Many local swimming centres offer PADI qualifications.

Diving is a hazardous activity, as well as being physically and mentally demanding, so good health and fitness, together with an awareness of health and safety, are vital. Research this career well!

Contacts

HSE, Rose Court, 2 Southwark Bridge, London SE1 9HS
0845 345 0055   www.hse.gov.uk

PADI
www.padi.com

Ecologist

If you've read a newspaper article about the bat or frog population and the challenge of maintaining the numbers of various species, then you already know something about what is involved in the work of an ecologist. This job can be covered by a number of job titles and may even overlap with other jobs in conservation, but in general terms, ecologists will be involved in studying plants, animals and their habitats. The aim of ecological work is to protect the natural environment from the possible damage caused by humans. Ecologists might also specialise in particular areas of conservation such as marine life, coastal areas or particular species of animals or plants.

The Job Description

Most ecologists are involved in some kind of habitat surveying, the creation and restoration of particular habitats, or ecological monitoring. This can include data collection and information gathering, impact assessments, research into animal behaviour, work on the population dynamics of species and analysis of ecosystems. In principal, ecologists are the experts that a range of organisations will consult when development of land is considered – they will advise on sustainable development. They can be involved in monitoring pollution, and advise on rare or protected species. Work can be with universities, research institutes funded by the Natural Environment Research Council, government agencies like the Environment Agency, museums or for charities such as the Royal Society for the Protection of Birds (RSPB).

The Person Specification

Competition for employment in ecological posts is tough, so general qualities like commitment and perseverance are needed. In addition, you will need good qualifications in biological or environmental subjects and a thorough knowledge of how natural systems function. You will need to be:

- passionate about animal and plant biology and knowledgeable about their classifications
- fascinated by living organisms
- able to enthuse others about the natural world
- able to pay attention to detail when doing field work which may be repetitive and tedious
- objective and methodical to be able to conduct scientific surveys.

What It Takes

The majority of applicants for these posts have strong scientific or environmental A levels/Diploma and degree-level qualifications in environmental/ecological subjects. The majority of university courses offer opportunities for field work, often in exotic locations, or exchange schemes with overseas universities which would allow you to gain a wider range of experience and knowledge. Many applicants for ecological jobs also need specialist postgraduate qualifications, proving expertise in specialist areas like zoology or regeneration work or species and habitat management.

What Else

Most people who are successful at gaining employment in this field have proved their commitment through voluntary or short-term contract work on environmental field projects. First job postings can often be as scientific officers for government agencies or water authorities, or as a field or ecological assistant.

What It Pays

There are many different employers in this field, but typically starting salaries are around £20,000–£24,000 per year. Keep up to date with job roles and salary scales through looking at job adverts in *New Scientist* and *Nature* magazines.

Prospects

Career paths in this line of work can lead to jobs such as head of plant ecology in a museum, to work as a general manager for the Environment Agency, to conservation work in the media, to research or teaching. It is worth checking out exciting employers such as 'The British Antarctic Survey' which advertises for field assistants for nine- or eighteen-month contracts to work in the polar environment doing important research. The work would be challenging and you would need to be able to cope with extreme climatic conditions but the experience could significantly help your future career.

Best Advice

It is worth becoming a student member of the British Ecological Society in order to gain access to special conferences and courses and to keep yourself well informed. Offer to volunteer for the RSPB, for natural history societies or for wildlife trusts. It is also important to have good computer skills, including knowledge of Geographical Information Systems. Most university courses offer a grounding in field work and computer information systems. Expedition skills such as Duke of Edinburgh awards and extreme sports experience or mountaineering skills are also valuable for accessing remote or challenging habitats.

Contacts

The British Ecological Society, 26 Blades Court, Putney, London SW15 2NU
020 8871 9797   www.britishecologicalsociety.org

The Institute of Ecology and Environmental Management, 45 Southgate
Street, Winchester, Hampshire SO23 9EH
01962 868626   www.ieem.org.uk

National Environment Research Council
www.nerc.ac.uk

The British Antarctic Survey
www.antarctica.ac.uk

Educational Psychologist

Educational psychologists are experts in the learning, behaviour and emotional development of children and young people and use this expertise to support children, their teachers and parents by helping them overcome problems that might stop them from achieving their full potential. By using their knowledge of psychological theories, current research and ways of assessing children, they can recommend the best techniques to support and motivate children or young people who are experiencing problems of one kind or another.

The Job Description

Educational psychologists will normally be involved when the school, or parents and carers, have noticed a problem, which might be to do with behaviour or with learning. For example, a primary school child might be struggling to read despite support, and a teacher might suspect dyslexia and request an assessment by the educational psychologist. Another child might appear to have a very short attention span and be displaying extremely disruptive behaviour in class. Again, an educational psychologist might be called in to assess this child in order to determine the best way to deal with the situation.

The first stage of the work is often this assessment stage, when educational psychologists would usually meet the child and parents/carers to discuss the problem. They might then arrange to observe the child in class and/or use short tests, which can help identify particular learning problems. This would also involve information gathering from a range of people who are in contact with that child. As a result of this assessment process, they could then make recommendations which might generate a referral for support with special educational needs, which is used to plan and fund the help that the child will need in school.

The Person Specification

As you can guess, educational psychologists need to have a wide range of skills and abilities to do this job well. They have to be able to build rapport with children easily, explain the purpose of tests in an unthreatening way, listen to parents/carers and teachers to gather information and advise/counsel them, and be able to make strong recommendations on techniques and strategies, which will be customised to each child's particular problem. For this work you would need to be:

- a good communicator, listener and report writer
- analytical, objective and logical when looking at test results
- confident about making specific recommendations to parents and teachers

- sensitive when offering advice to teachers/parents
- prepared to undertake specialised training.

What It Takes

This is a degree-only profession and you will need to gain an accredited British Psychological Society (BPS) degree in Psychology as a first step – this will also need to provide the Graduate Basis for Registration (GBR) to ensure you can apply for the next stage of the training required. To gain a place on a psychology degree, you will normally need five GCSEs, C grade and above, or equivalent, and two to three A levels/Diploma or equivalent. Some psychology degrees may ask for an A level in maths as there is normally a strong mathematical/statistical/analytical component to psychology degrees. Check www.ucas.com for exact A level points and subject choice requirements for specific psychology degrees. Be very careful in choosing your course so that you are certain that it is BPS accredited and provides GBR.

The degree stage is just the first step. You will need to aim to get a 2.i or First Class Honours degree classification and then gain at least one year's full-time experience working with children or young people; this could be in a school as a teaching assistant or as a learning support assistant or in youth work of some kind. Without this vital experience and contact with children/young people, you will not be able to apply for the next stage of professional training.

You would next need to enter the extremely competitive annual application process for a three-year accredited training course for educational psychologists, leading to a doctorate. This programme involves study for the first year at university; then in the second and third years you would work three or four days per week for an educational psychology service under the supervision of a qualified educational psychologist, while completing your studies. This course is run at about a dozen universities and the on-line process is controlled by the Children's Workforce Development Council (CWDC). Competition is intense for places on these courses and applicants need to show commitment to the profession and academic capability. In Scotland the system is slightly different – you would take a two-year Master's in educational psychology. Ultimately, after all this hard work and training, you will be a Doctor of Educational Psychology (or Master of Educational Psychology in Scotland) and eligible to apply for chartered psychologist status.

What Else

None of this will put you off if you like the idea of really making a difference to a child's achievements and development, especially as educational psychologists play an important part in training teachers and other professionals to deal with behaviour problems in the classroom and issues such as bullying. You may also get the chance to do important research into methods of teaching and motivating children, or be valuable to schools in your role as an educational consultant.

Nonetheless, it is worth realising that while there is a current shortage of educational psychologists and therefore good career opportunities for qualified professionals, you will need to be very certain that this is the right career for you, and have determination to motivate yourself through the academic and experience-based requirements for this career and its training route.

What It Pays
Typical starting salaries for newly qualified chartered educational psychologists are in the range £30,546–£40,111 per year, and while most educational psychologists work in local government for education departments, freelance consultancy work is also possible and offers the potential for higher earnings.

Prospects
There are opportunities for research, consultancy and training work associated with this profession, as expertise in the areas of behaviour and learning is highly sought after by schools, colleges, charities and voluntary organisations.

Best Advice
Be really sure that you are committed to working with children, and other professionals, and have the interpersonal skills and scientific interest in the causes of behaviour and learning problems. Any experience as a volunteer in schools would be valuable, especially supporting a child with special educational needs. Playscheme work during summer vacations with charities like Barnardos would also be good background experience. The BPS website is an excellent source of good information.

Contacts
British Psychological Society, St Andrews House, 48 Princess Road East, Leicester LE1 7DR
0116 254 9568   www.bps.org.uk

Association of Educational Psychologists (AEP)
www.aep.org.uk

Barnardos
www.barnardos.org.uk

CWDC
www.cwdcouncil.org.uk/educational-psychology

Emergency Medical Dispatcher

Emergency medical dispatchers work in an emergency control room and make sure that a call for help through the 999 system is dealt with efficiently and promptly, and that an ambulance is quickly sent to someone who requires assistance. Dispatchers have to be able to deal with the initial call, taking essential details about the person's condition and location and deciding on the best course of action.

The Job Description

The first stage of this role is call handling; invariably members of the public who phone 999 are stressed and worried and they need to be carefully questioned in a precise way to obtain the essential details. It may be a call from a GP, the police or fire service or a person at the scene of an accident. Dispatchers have to be able to quickly assess the level of need and determine the best response. They might refer the caller to another service or arrange for an ambulance to be sent. Alternatively, they may have responsibility for the dispatch of a rapid response car or even a paramedic helicopter.

The Person Specification

Dispatchers have to maintain a calm approach when callers are extremely frightened or even angry. They have to be able to interact well on the phone and take responsibility for what might be life and death decisions. They cannot be seen to waste expensive resources or send out ambulances unnecessarily. You would need to be:

- interested in health and emergency situations
- willing and able to handle pressure and responsibility
- a good communicator over the phone
- able to pay attention to detail
- quick at making decisions and assessing potential risk
- prepared to take intensive training in first-aid, the work of accident and emergency and radio communications
- knowledgeable about local geography/locations.

What It Takes

Ambulance services across the UK may have varying requirements for control room staff but, as a rule, a good general education and keyboard skills are needed and preferably GCSEs in English, maths and a science or equivalent. A knowledge of medical terms, map reading and the local area of that ambulance service is obviously useful, and community-language skills could be especially important. Intensive training is offered to trainee dispatchers both in a training centre and on the job, under supervision.

You will learn how to use the switchboard, how to give telephone advice and how to use the computerised systems to log calls.

What Else
Experienced dispatchers may have to talk to a caller and take them through a procedure to resuscitate someone or to deliver a baby.

What It Pays
The NHS starting salary for this role is £12,577 per year.

Prospects
There are opportunities to progress into supervision and training of control room staff, or to become a control room manager. Other emergency services such as the police and fire service have their own call control rooms so you could move into other services.

Best Advice
Get involved with the St John Ambulance – www.sja.org.uk – and take a first-aid course. Work hard at sciences and try hospital volunteering at your local NHS hospital. Find out if your local ambulance service has a First Responder voluntary service – First Responder volunteers are trained to respond to emergency situations in their neighbourhood area.

Contacts
The British Paramedics Association, 28 Wilfrid Street, Derby DE23 8GF
01332 746356   www.britishparamedic.org

NHS Careers
www.nhscareers.nhs.uk

The Ambulance Service Association
www.nhsconfed.org/ambulance-trusts

Event Management

Event and conference management has developed from the hospitality, exhibitions and public relations areas into a career in its own right. It combines aspects of PR and marketing with customer service and hospitality management. Event managers have to be skilled at organising projects such as conferences, seminars, exhibitions and award ceremonies. They are responsible for every detail, from promotion to venue, speaker booking to the budgeting and costing of events, and, finally, to the hands-on organisation of a conference, ensuring the smooth running of the event.

The Job Description

For all sorts of reasons, organisations will require events or conferences for training, dissemination of information, marketing and promotion or simply as incentives for the sales force. These could be half-day or all-day events or longer, and although some companies may hand over the organisation of such events to a member of staff, large companies frequently contract it out to a specialist event management company. The role could involve arranging a medical conference for doctors, organising a political party conference or running a training event.

Initially, an event manager will meet the client to determine the exact brief, that is, what the client has in mind and any preferences for venue or cost that they might express. Once this analysis is completed, the event manager will conduct a venue search, negotiate hotel or conference venue pricing and liaise with the client to make recommendations. When this has been agreed, the real organisation of the event starts. From this point on, the event manager will be responsible for promoting the event to possible delegates, making room bookings, organising catering (including any special dietary needs of delegates), arranging audio-visual services for presenters and dealing with overall bookings from delegates or the organisation.

The Person Specification

As you might expect from the job description, an event manager has to be multi-skilled and able to deal with a range of people (including delegates, the client organisation, caterers, audio-visual technicians and conference staff) in the most effective way. The job can be desk based for part of the time, but is also likely to involve a considerable amount of travel. You would need to be:

- an excellent communicator, both verbally and in writing
- a good leader with excellent team work skills
- able to take the initiative and deal with problems and potential crises

- skilled at administration, with a broad range of IT skills including Microsoft Word, Excel and the use of databases
- possibly experienced in hospitality and catering at some level, but certainly able to deal with catering details
- able to understand and use audio-visual and presentation skills to support speakers and make proposals to clients yourself
- able to deal with financial costings and budgets
- able to speak foreign languages for overseas conferences.

What It Takes

There is not really a set route into this career, but frequently event managers have taken hospitality management degrees or Foundation degree courses, or have undertaken training on the job (possibly after A level/Diploma or BTEC qualifications) with large hotel groups. Alternatively, any business training or degree could lead into this work, especially on the marketing or PR side.

There are a few courses that allow specialisation in event management as a specific module or even throughout the degree. An example of this is the Events Management degree course at Leeds Metropolitan University, but research on the UCAS website (www.ucas.com) will give you further information on suitable or similar courses. It may be possible to gain an administration job with an event management company and work your way up, or enter event management after experience in hotels and restaurants. Specialist university courses do cover the full range of this work and often offer sandwich years or vacation placements to help you gain on-the-ground experience.

What Else

Be prepared to deal with any eventuality in this job and combine practical skills with a creative approach when required. Attention to detail is highly regarded in this job and makes the difference between good and mediocre events. Work hours can be regular or very unsocial, depending on whether you are working at the planning or delivery stage of the event.

What It Pays

Pay varies across the UK and for overseas conferences, but trainee event managers may start on £14,000–£21,000 per year.

Prospects

Event management is more developed in the USA as a career, so there are prospects for work abroad. Some managers go on to specialise further in the incentives management side of the industry, where companies reward staff, and sometimes their partners, with exotic conferences in order to encourage future profits. At the razzmatazz end of the industry, there are the political party and fundraising conferences featuring colourful special effects and audio-visual tricks.

Sports event management involving client entertainment at big sporting events is a further area of specialisation – think of strawberries and cream in the VIP tent at the Wimbledon Championships. This area of corporate hospitality is a growth area and has links with the incentives management area, as companies want to reward their customers and encourage future business through wining and dining them at Ascot or the British Golf Open. Though glamorous in appearance, these events are the result of the hard work and meticulous planning skills of event management companies or consultants.

Best Advice

As a student try and get involved in running student events, booking bands or even being entertainments secretary. Vacation work at prestigious corporate hospitality events, waiting on tables or doing bar work would be great on-the-ground experience for your CV.

IT skills and office experience are also vital. It is worth doing your research through the Association of Conferences and Events to get a real world idea of the industry.

Contacts

Check the universities' UCAS site (www.ucas.com) for courses in event management, marketing or public relations.

Chartered Institute of Marketing, Moor Hall, Maidenhead, Berkshire SL6 9QH
01628 427500   www.cim.co.uk

Association of Conferences and Events
www.martex.co.uk/ace

Corporate Event Service
www.cesbook.co.uk

Event Magazine
www.eventmagazine.co.uk

Family Court Adviser

Family court advisers are employed by a government department called CAFCASS (the Children and Families Court Advisory Support Service) to support children who are involved in family court proceedings which often happen due to divorce and family conflict. As you can imagine, appearing in court can be a stressful business for adults – for children it can be incredibly daunting and possibly damaging. Advisers meet the children involved and make reports and recommendations to the courts, based on their assessment of what is best for an individual child.

The Job Description

Family court advisers ensure that, throughout a legal process, the needs and welfare of a child or children in a family are protected and that their opinions on preferences and custody are considered. They have to represent to the court what the wishes and feelings of the child might be. They might appoint a solicitor specifically to represent the child's viewpoint and have to be objective in the way that they investigate what is happening to the child as a result of the court proceedings, and encourage co-operation by both parents and any other parties. They have to understand child development and be able to engage with children, putting them at their ease.

The Person Specification

This is in fact a specialism of social work, so advisers need to be qualified social workers who want to work in a legal context and have a natural ability to communicate with all ages of children. To do this work you would need to be:

- able to be impartial and sensitive to the needs of children
- able to deal with difficult situations and conflicts
- a good communicator with adults and children
- a good negotiator
- aware of the legal obligation which social workers have to protect children from physical or psychological harm.

What It Takes

For this work you would need to be a fully qualified social worker with at least three years' experience in social work. You would first need to study for a social work degree which would include placements in social work agencies. To study for a social work degree you would need to have a good GCSE profile or equivalent, with C grades and over in maths and English, and A levels/Diploma in subjects such as sociology, law, psychology or health and social care.

What Else

Advisers have to work with a range of other agencies and when they investigate a case, they will consult teachers, school nurses and other support services to gain the full picture of the circumstances of a child. The challenge of this role is that advisers influence decisions made by the courts.

What It Pays

Starting salaries for experienced social workers who move into this work are currently in the range £28,869–£34,643 per year.

Prospects

Family court advisers can move into other social work specialisms such as fostering and adoption or child protection work or into management roles.

Best Advice

Study law and understand the work of the courts. Try and gain work experience with a social worker within a social services department.

Contacts

General Social Care Council, Goldings House, 2 Hay's Lane, London SE1 2HB
020 7397 5800   www.gscc.org.uk

Social Care and Social Work Careers Information website
www.socialworkcareers.co.uk

CAFCASS
www.cafcass.gov.uk

Fashion Buyer

Often working a year in advance, buyers consult with designers on
fashion trends so that they can predict which garments they ought to buy
for stores on the High Street. They have to keep themselves well informed
about catwalk trends and gather information about styles and designs,
including predicting possible directions for prints and fabrics. Going
abroad to Europe or New York to source designs is a particularly attractive
aspect of this job.

The Job Description
Buyers have to make decisions on products and ranges according to their
hunches about what will be popular or on trend. Sometimes they work
with in-house design teams; at other times they work with suppliers –
checking out design sketches and fabric swatches. They need to be up to
date on colour themes and key trends for the product range they cover.
They are also responsible for the quality and finish of garments or fashion
accessories they purchase/order. They have to be alert to sudden style
changes or trends, which can be triggered by something a celebrity wears
at a film premiere or by TV or music videos. They also have to be aware of
the potential market for what they buy and negotiate the price with the
designer/supplier.

The Person Specification
You will need a passion for fashion, an eye for design and trends and
a strong head for business and the retail industry. Stores will take a
gamble by selling designs that you purchase and will lose money if your
predictions are incorrect. You will need to be:

- creative, with a good eye for colour, texture, fabrics
- able to cope with a fast-moving environment and work under pressure
- fascinated by fashion and good design
- flexible and organised
- technically aware of how garments are made and put together.

What It Takes
Most buyers have a fashion, retail or business degree; there are some
excellent degree courses at university fashion colleges which offer a
real grounding in marketing and trend awareness for this work. After
graduation you would probably start training through a retail or store
management or buyer scheme, which offers specific training for this work.
Most buyers start their careers as a buyer's admin assistant – these are
sought-after roles as they are often the best starting point for a career as
a buyer. The next career step would be to become a buyer's assistant and
then hopefully this would ensure career progression to a buyer's role.

It is possible to work up to a buyer's job through work as a retail assistant, followed by a move to an administrative role in the head office of a retail group.

Some buyers further their training through the Chartered Institute of Purchasing and Supply (CIPS) qualifications.

What Else

This is a dream job for many design or fashion students, so there are plenty of talented applicants. Determination and motivation will be needed to gain entry to buyer training schemes. While in the future you may want to work for a big-name store, your first role might be with a supermarket or mass-market fashion brand. Many jobs are based in London with well-known retail groups or department stores.

What It Pays

Average salaries are around £18,000–£19,000 per year for London-based companies.

Prospects

Buyers can progress into production management, fashion forecasting or even work abroad in other fashion capitals such as Rome or Paris.

Best Advice

On your shopping trips, analyse how trends develop. Read the top-quality fashion magazines like *Vogue* and *Elle*. The industry magazine is *Drapers*, and a subscription would be potentially useful, as it would keep you up to date with current industry topics and would allow you to check out the jobs advertised.

Develop your own style and skills in predicting future trends. Textiles A level/diploma would give you a good grounding for a career in the industry and make sure you research the best fashion- or textile-related university courses. A retail fashion part-time job is an ideal way of gaining experience of the retailing side of this sector and will look good on future applications for buyer work.

Contacts

Chartered Institute of Purchasing and Supply, Easton House, Easton on the Hill, Stamford, Lincs PE9 3NZ
01780 756777   www.cips.org

Check large retail group websites such as
www.arcadiagroup.co.uk or www.next.co.uk

Drapers
www.drapersonline.com

Fashion Stylist

The whole look of a fashion magazine and its layouts, or a music video, for example, is controlled by a fashion stylist who works with a photographer to produce the designed look. They decide on models, the hairstyles, make-up and accessories and are responsible for decisions about lighting and the set. Their work normally relies on their contacts and having a good agent who recommends them for work on fashion or video shoots. Some stylists work for magazines as part of the editorial team that puts together the fashion pages.

The Job Description

Stylists can be tasked with creating the style or image for a magazine shoot or with taking care of the detail like obtaining the garments or props or the best merchandise to display. They may work with designers to promote their work, organising and 'casting' for a catwalk show and ensuring that the look of a fashion collection is what the designer wants and that the style will be effectively promoted. They have to take into account what their client wants and the budget for that shoot, and might be working on an advert, a pop video or a fashion show. They may have to source accessories or designs to fit with an overall theme and look.

They may start with a design brief from the magazine editor or a client; then they will research, shop for, hire or loan merchandise or props needed to create the look required. They will work with photographers, lighting technicians and even coordinate the building of a set.

Those stylists who work for magazines may also write the copy for articles that go with the fashion photos. Freelance stylists are very dependent on a succession of contracts, and rely on contacts for future work and repeat business. Styling celebrities for a big event might be possible but you will need to have established a reputation and have a great contacts book which you protect and guard. Your contacts might be young and upcoming designers, fabric warehouses, underwear companies or theatrical or film agents.

The Person Specification

Successful stylists often have magazine editorial experience along with keen fashion sense and an interest in media, film, TV and music. As a freelancer they will work from contract to contract – for the best stylists this could mean a day's work that earns £10,000. However, they have to put up with long working hours and an uncertain earning capacity, especially at the start of their careers. Many have to establish quite exclusive working relationships with photographers who rely on the stylist to deal with the detail to free them up to focus on the technical aspects of their photography. They also have to coordinate the models, public relations staff and pay attention to fine details, such as a hem that has fallen down or a bra strap that is showing. You would need to be:

- gifted at finding props and merchandise for shoots
- enthusiastic about fashion, aware of trends and how to put together a look or style
- confident about approaching possible contacts for work and good at making an impression
- determined and motivated to break into what is a popular and competitive profession
- imaginative and creative to come up with new ideas
- observant and pay attention to detail
- a strong communicator.

What It Takes

It may be that you have to work for free on a magazine or with a photographer at the outset to get some credibility and experience. You may have to gain experience in fashion retail first or make friends with new and upcoming designers. For stylist work on a magazine most start by working on short projects free of charge to gain experience and develop the specific knowledge needed.

University degrees in fashion design or textiles or even fashion journalism or styling (see www.ucas.com and London College of Fashion (LCF)) can be an advantage. You will need A levels/Diploma or equivalent including a creative subject such as art, textiles or photography as a first step. You will then find that you need at least a portfolio of examples of your work and possibly a Foundation art BTEC qualification to gain a place on the popular fashion- or design-oriented university courses.

For magazine work, a magazine journalism qualification could help but you need to be confident that you can write too – the London College of Fashion offers a degree, for example, in Fashion Journalism. An A level in English is generally required for journalism courses.

Interestingly some courses are being developed for the stylist side of the work and the Foundation degree in Fashion Styling and Photography (LCF) may be worth considering.

In addition there are introductory short courses offered by LCF and Central St Martin's College of Art and Design which, for a relatively small cost, offer an insight into the work; short courses may be five days long or offered over three Saturdays. These are perfect for those who are doing work experience with a magazine and want to boost their skills.

What Else

Over and above possible qualifications, it would seem that the ability to be outgoing and deal with pressure is vital. Most stylists are practical and resourceful; patience and a sense of humour might be the best qualities for dealing with the potentially difficult people and situations you will encounter. Dressmaking skills may be a useful extra and you could start now to put together your stylist kit which will include an assortment of useful bits and pieces such as pins, tape, needles and threads and a clothes steamer.

What It Pays

Salary details are problematic because of the freelance nature of this work and depending on who will employ you. You could expect in the region of £14,000–£23,000 per year for your first job on a magazine and freelance rates will be dependent on how popular you are.

Prospects

Stylist work with more regular hours and a steady salary might be available through the personal shopper role offered by major retail stores.

Best Advice

Retail experience in buying or merchandising can help you build your network of contacts. Research how fashion magazines and adverts create their look. Get any work experience you can on a magazine by sending your CV to named fashion editors.

Contacts

UK Fashion Exports and the British Clothing Industry Association, 5 Portland Place, London W1B 1PW
020 7636 5577   www.ukfashionexports.com

London College of Fashion and Central St Martin's College of Art and Design, University of the Arts, London
www.fashion.arts.ac.uk

Film/TV Director

The director is the person on a film or TV set who decides exactly how the programme or film will be developed based on the requirements of the script or the programme brief. This means bringing together every aspect of the whole process, including the crew, actors and technical staff, choice of locations, design of the sets, right through to the final production.

The Job Description

In some ways the director has to have an incredibly wide range of skills, including an ability to deal with both performers and technical crew, as well as the filmic techniques required to bring the script or brief to completion on budget and deadline. Decisions about scripts or programmes, and the best way to produce them, are all the responsibility of the director. They have to have a clear vision for what will be created and the management skills to lead a diverse team of personalities through the production process, right through to post-production.

The Person Specification

Directors often have experience behind the camera, in research or in editing, and they have to know enough about other people's jobs so that they can motivate them to a great performance or to produce the best lighting or sound or design. In films, they have to be able to talk to the scriptwriter about the script and interpret it in the most meaningful way. For this work you would need to be:

- able to work with lots of differently talented people
- prepared to gain experience in any area of film and TV
- able to work under pressure
- good at managing and leading a team
- extremely well organised and persistent
- creative with technical skills.

What It Takes

Most film directors have either worked up through editing or technical roles in TV or film and/or have studied film at film school, college or university. Some directors start off in video production and then move into film. You will need to check accredited and recommended courses of study through Skillset, which accredits courses through its Screen Academies. You can also check the National Film and Television School, which often needs volunteers to be crew on student films. Make sure the course you choose offers you the chance to actually make films as part of a film crew.

Regardless of training or experience, your first job will be as a runner on a film set – most directors start here (see page 185).

What Else

Check the popular production schemes offered by the BBC and consider applying for talent schemes and competitions offered, such as BBC Talent and Channel 4. Although competition is fierce, this is an extremely valuable way to get into this industry. FT2 offers a paid work-based route into freelance film work with technical and production schemes lasting up to two years, including up to four six-month placements with different film or TV production companies. Again, there is tough competition for places on these schemes so make sure you gain any experience you can while at college and start creating your own film ideas.

The BBC holds competitions for new filmmakers which sometimes result in paid placements in their film production units. Channel 4 does something similar through their Small Wonders scheme.

What It Pays

Good directors can name their own price, but pay varies according to type of production and experience required. The production trainee scheme offered by the BBC offers a starting salary of £19,000 per year.

Prospects

Some directors move into work as a producer or actually write and produce/direct their own scripts.

Best Advice

Get a job as a runner on a film or TV set. Work for free as part of the film crew for a production. Check the FT2 New Entrant Technical Training Scheme – a funded training programme for entry to careers in editing, camera work, production and sound. Both the BBC and Channel 4 advertise places on work experience schemes on their websites.

Contacts

Skillset, Focus Point, 21 Caledonian Road, London N1 9GB
020 7713 9800   www.skillset.org/careers

BBC
www.bbc.co.uk/talent or www.bbc.co.uk/workexperience

Channel 4
www.channel4.com/4careers

National Film and Television School
www.nftsfilm-tv.ac.uk

FT2
www.ft2.org.uk

Fish Farmer

This may be a career idea that has never occurred to you, but if you want an outdoor career and find fishing interesting, then this might be the right job for you. Much of the fish we eat is not caught out in the deep blue sea or in rivers, but is bred specifically in fish farms. A fish farmer breeds and rears fish for food and for private ornamental garden ponds or for sports fishermen to catch. The job of the fish farmer can be varied according to the size of the operation; some fish farmers will be mainly involved with hatchery work while others might do that as well as actually managing the production, including sales and delivery to buyers.

The Job Description

Most fish farms are small, so staff can be involved in a range of operations; these might include outdoor work, feeding the fish from spawning time to harvest, cleaning ponds and pools to maintain the perfect habitat, caring for the health of the fish, harvesting, sorting and grading the fish. In addition, managers of fish farms might manage the hatchery workers doing these outdoor duties as well as being involved in marketing the fish product through wholesalers or supermarkets. Some fish farms may also be involved in smoking the fish or offer fishing facilities to local angling groups.

The Person Specification

To do this kind of work, you need to be the kind of person who wants an outdoor and active countryside job. This can involve possibly good conditions in the summer months, but less pleasant conditions in the winter. You will probably be directly involved in breeding fish, then be responsible for feeding them – perhaps by hand or through an automatic machine which you fill. You will need to keep the fish healthy by checking the water, treating it when necessary, and testing the temperature and oxygen levels.

In addition, you would work longer hours in the spring when the initial rearing of the fish occurs. Typically you would work various shifts which might include early mornings, evenings and weekends. You would need to be:

- physically fit and active
- interested in fish and being part of a growth area of the fish industry
- able to work well as part of a team
- able to pay attention to detail
- ready to work in sometimes remote locations
- prepared to work long hours, which can mean weekend work.

What It Takes

Many agricultural colleges offer various courses in fish farming, such as the BTEC First and National Diplomas in Fish Farming. For these courses GCSE passes or equivalent are required and these may lead to first jobs on a fish farm. Some people train in the job and gain qualifications through an NVQ in Fish Husbandry at Level 2. It may also be possible to get a first job (without previous training) and train on the job for this work.

At a higher level, aspiring fish farm managers might take university courses in marine and/or freshwater biology, which might cover fish farming – see www.ucas.com for courses. The Institute of Fisheries Management also offers a Diploma in Fisheries Management.

What Else

Jobs tend to be available in remote areas such as Scotland and North Yorkshire.

What It Pays

Starting salaries can be around £11,000 per year, with managers being able to earn up to £30,000 per year.

Prospects

Self-employment or freelance cover work to fish farms might be possible, and other work opportunities might be possible in rivers management with local councils or with the Environment Agency.

Best Advice

Get to know a lot about fishing and learn about fish. Join an angling society. Try some work experience on a fish farm.

Contacts

Institute of Fisheries Management, 22 Rushworth Avenue, West Bridgford, Nottingham NG2 7LF
01115 982 2317   www.ifm.org.uk

The Environment Agency
www.environment-agency.gov.uk

Flood Defence Engineer/ Officer/Planner

There have been times lately when the news has been full of flood incidents in different parts of the country, so the work involved in flood defence has possibly had a higher profile than in previous years. The natural environment that we live in has always been unpredictable, so effective flood defence and planning can protect people and property from the challenging problems nature can throw at us. Flood defence engineers and planners aim to develop effective flood defences, and must be good at risk management decision making.

The Job Description

Flood defence engineers and planners are involved in the co-ordination and maintenance of programmes and flood defence projects. They use their knowledge of river or coastal engineering to supervise projects, deal with environmental consultants, assess and inspect defences and monitor expenditure. Their aim is to reduce the risk of flooding through the management of flood maintenance programmes and flood-risk mapping.

The Person Specification

Flood defence engineers and planners have to have a good working knowledge of flood defence and river/coastal engineering. They would be involved in the design and construction of flood defence schemes, working proactively to prevent incidents or disasters. They regularly assess and draft projections of danger spots and are the key players when, despite their efforts, floods occur. They often use computer-aided design (CAD) and geographical information systems (GIS) software to draw plans and make projections. You would have to be:

- an excellent communicator to deal with consultants, maintenance workers and technical staff
- IT literate, with specialist data management skills, as collection of data informs the decisions that have to be made
- good at supervising and managing in a team situation
- able to make sound and objective decisions
- able to write detailed reports
- committed to maintaining and improving flood protection
- able to prioritise expenditure on flood defence according to national and regional budgets.

What It Takes

Flood defence engineers normally have qualifications in civil engineering at degree level as well as on-the-ground experience through work placements. Planners may be engineers or environmental/data managers and they may have degrees in environmental or data management subjects, normally with knowledge of geographical information systems (GIS) software and Microsoft Excel and Access.

For civil engineering degrees A levels/Diploma in maths and physics or BTEC/vocational qualifications in construction or engineering are normally required. Planners may have geography or environmental science A levels with maths or sciences, possibly even computer science. Many courses offer a sandwich or placement year where you would take paid work in water/civil engineering or environmental management to gain additional experience.

What Else

Most engineers work towards chartered civil engineer or incorporated engineer status.

What It Pays

Starting salaries can be around £19,500–£23,000 per year.

Prospects

The main employer is the Environment Agency, but there are increasing opportunities overall and with environmental consultancies. Work overseas is also possible with charities such as WaterAid. There are predictions that there will be a significantly increasing demand for engineers over the next few years.

Best Advice

Try and organise any kind of environmental work experience, preferably with a firm of civil engineers.

Contacts

The Civil Engineering Careers Service, The Institution of Civil Engineers, 1 Great George Street, London SW1P 3AA
020 7222 7722   www.ice.org.uk

The Environment Agency
www.environment-agency.gov.uk

Institute of Environmental Management and Assessment (IEEMA)
www.ieema.net

WaterAid
www.wateraid.org.uk

Food Stylist

You may have seen a mouth-watering TV advert with delicious food or you may have noticed the food photos next to the recipes in a cookery book or magazine; it's very exacting photography to ensure food looks perfect, and it is the job of the food stylist to ensure that it does for the photo shoot. Food stylists use different techniques to prepare food arrangements for the photographer and they also arrange food for chefs, buffets and weddings so that customers are tempted to eat the food provided and return to that restaurant/hotel again.

The Job Description
Food stylists can work with chefs when they are devising menus, deciding on the perfect presentation for each recipe. They know how to create eye-pleasing designs which convince customers of the quality of the food, even before they taste it. They may also work on cruise ships or for wedding planners or hotels, or they can work for TV programmes, advertising agencies or cookery book publishers. They have to make sure that food is created in the first place according to the requirements of the customer and then they present it so that it appears fresh and appetising. They have to be able to cook well but they may also create food or ice sculptures that catch the interest of diners. They use an array of equipment including regular cooking intensils, as well as blow torches to brown a piece of vegetable or meat, tweezers to move a fine particle of rice, fine brushes to deposit oil on a carrot or a water spray to prevent food from drying out under strong photographic lights.

The Person Specification
Stylists have to be qualified chefs with a passionate interest in food. They have to be able to design and create appealing recipes which look as good as they taste. They have to be able to work with the chefs, photographers, restaurant owners and agencies who employ them and come up with innovative ideas for presenting recipes using props and settings. You would need to be:

- gifted with food preparation and willing to train as a chef
- creative, with a good eye for detail
- aware of the technical side of food photography
- practical and good at problem solving
- able to interact well with all kinds of people.

What It Takes
Most stylists start by training through a catering course and through qualifying as a chef. You could do this through a City & Guilds Catering course, taking NVQ Level 1, 2 and 3 or equivalent either full time at

college or through an apprenticeship and day release to college. Some people take a private Cordon Bleu type of course and then train to be a stylist. You will need a good general education, preferably with GCSEs or equivalent, in English, maths and science to gain entry to courses.

Once you have qualified, you will need to gain one to two years' experience as a chef before you will have enough experience to apply for a job as a food stylist assistant. There will be strong competition for jobs with food stylists but this is the best way to train. The University of Central Lancashire has an MA in Food Styling by distance learning which may be worth considering.

What Else
While artistic flair is needed, a practical attitude and the creativity to come up with new ideas of presentation is vital. Most stylists work on a freelance basis from contract to contract.

What It Pays
Food stylist assistants normally start on a daily rate of £80 per day but this can increase once trained to £200 per day or more, depending on types of work undertaken.

Prospects
Some stylists work for food companies, while others form creative alliances with certain chefs who rely on them for presentation advice. The popularity of TV food programmes means that there is increasing demand for stylists.

Best Advice
Work hard at food technology at school and take an interest in cookery and food. Start to notice photos in cookery books and analyse how they are presented. Try and gain some experience with hotels who specialise in big-event catering – pick up tips on how they present the food.

Contacts
People 1st, 2nd Floor, Armstrong House, 38 Market Square, Uxbridge UB8 1LH.
0870 060 2550   www.people1st.co.uk

Cordon Bleu School
www.lcblondon.com

University of Central Lancashire MA in Food Styling
www.uclan.ac.uk/courses/pg

Football Scout

This may seem a dream job to many keen footballers who either haven't made it as professional footballers or are keen football supporters. The truth is that, dream or not, it is still about painstaking, hard work and standing about on football pitches on cold, windy days, hoping to discover the next Wayne Rooney. Typically, a football scout may cover a geographical area of 25 to 40 miles, but he or she will have to tramp every football pitch in that area. Practically speaking, they are used to source young talent, so they are likely to be a spectator at many under-11 football games at school or club level. Knowing the territory and making good contacts are a key part of this job.

Big clubs may also employ a chief scout who is involved in sourcing new players and talent. There are only a handful of these chief scout positions and they generally go to retired footballers or coaches.

The Job Description

In the search for talented footballers, the scout has to watch competitive school soccer, which might take place mainly in the evenings and at weekends. They have to know the full details of all the junior football leagues, inter-town games and fixtures. To do this they have to do their homework, contacting local education departments for details of schools in the area and the local football association for other fixtures. Once they have checked match reports in local newspapers and are totally familiar with the area, they need to make contact with key teachers and team managers, so that they get to hear about all competitions and school soccer events.

Increasingly, at club level, methods of sourcing players have become more sophisticated, with the use of software such as ProScout7, which tracks players all over the world and offers instant feedback to clubs on potential new stars and performance levels. This means that the stereotypical picture of a scout in a flat cap with a pen and pad may become less common. The scout might be taking digital photos and using a laptop and a software program to analyse performance or potential ability.

The Person Specification

Most scouts do this job for love, not money. They have to be determined to know their territory and be persistent in watching, monitoring and assessing players who may seem to have potential. Obviously they need an excellent knowledge of football, but they must also be able to spot football intelligence in young players. They will look for certain characteristics such as pace and speed, strength, 'touch' and technique, as well as temperament and commitment. They will probably feed back to club academies or schools of excellence unless they are producing data which the clubs access by computer whenever they want it. They will need to be CRB (Criminal Records Bureau) checked by the police because of their contact with children and young people. You would need to be:

- dedicated to spotting potential in young footballers
- skilled at analysing technique, 'touch' and ball skills
- prepared to go out regularly in all weathers and cover a good geographical area in your search
- encouraging and supportive of young players.

What It Takes

Unless you are working at the highest level, this may be a part-time or second job, often undertaken with passion but with minimal financial reward. Some scouts are former players and may have greater credibility with clubs if they have played at semi- or professional level, but most are just football enthusiasts who will go anywhere to watch a game of football.

What Else

Most scouts start on a voluntary basis, gaining knowledge of their area and then making contacts, perhaps with local clubs. These contacts, if nurtured, will provide them with leads to good young players. Typically, a PE teacher may phone a scout and encourage him/her to come down and watch a player. Once a scout knows their network of contacts and area, they may contact a club, asking if they can offer their services as a scout. At this stage, they would probably have the names of some promising players to suggest. On the basis of the success of these recommended players, a club may choose to use the scout again. So the role of the scout depends on the success of the young players who they put forward.

What It Pays

Typically, if a player, recommended by a scout, is signed by a club, then the scout will be paid a bonus or incentive, depending on the size and wealth of the club. Some scouts are also paid a small weekly amount, travelling expenses and a small amount for phone calls, postage, etc. Most do it for job satisfaction and because they love to be involved with football.

Prospects

For a scout with the golden touch, larger clubs and better opportunities might be available. It would be wise to familiarise yourself with the scouting software used and feed into the companies who promote this data.

Best Advice

Scouting needs a methodical approach and an ability to establish a network of contacts.

Contacts

The Football Association, 25 Soho Square, London W1D 4FA
www.the-fa.org

The Professional Footballers' Association
www.givemefootball.com

Scout7
www.scout7.com

Forensic Scientist

You've probably watched *CSI* or British forensic science-based TV programmes, and it's quite confusing to see the range of professionals involved in solving a case. There may be police investigators, crime scene investigators and then they may show someone in a lab inspecting a fibre, dog hair or tyre tread. The forensic scientist is generally this last person, the professional who supports the investigation through scientific analysis, often based in a laboratory. It may seem to be all blood, gore and exciting discoveries in crime investigation, but in reality it is often the painstaking and detailed testing of minute artefacts in a rigorous and often repetitive way with the aim of producing evidence in support of the prosecution of a case. Forensic science is clearly linked to the legal process and developments in this field have revolutionised the investigation of a range of cases.

Forensic scientists normally specialise in the investigation of crimes against property, such as burglaries or possible cases of arson, or in determining the cause of a potentially suspicious death.

The Job Description
Most forensic scientists work in laboratories, examining blood or tissue samples, or materials from the scene of the crime. They might analyse blood or urine samples for drink-driving cases, or may assess whether a person has used banned substances or drugs. Forensic scientists may attend the scene of a crime to collect data or samples. They have to make detailed notes and use many different technical instruments, including infra-red, microscopic and DNA testing equipment. As you would expect, it is a highly scientific, analytical job. In addition, forensic scientists may have to produce reports which may have to be presented in court.

The Person Specification
High scientific and numerical ability and interest is needed for this job, along with a determined, painstaking approach and great attention to detail. You would need to be:

- good at problem solving
- methodical and analytical
- able to make reasoned observations
- good at report writing
- comfortable in laboratory and scene of crime situations.

What It Takes

Most forensic science staff work for government or police labs, like the Forensic Science Service, a Home Office agency, or the Metropolitan Police Service Forensic Science Service, and jobs are normally at assistant forensic scientist and forensic scientist grade. This is a relatively small profession – there are about 11 government laboratories and other private companies offering forensic services, but the number of jobs is normally considerably fewer than the applicants wishing to land them. The Forensic Science Service may attract thousands of applications when they advertise so only those who have the right experience, skills and qualifications will make it through the application procedure.

In practice most people have at least A levels/Diploma in sciences for forensic science assistant posts, and degree or even Master's level qualifications for forensic scientist roles. Degree subject study can be varied – but there is a preference for degrees in biology, chemistry, biochemistry, pharmacology or possibly the newer forensic science degrees. Forensics degrees often offer simulation crime scenes for students to work on and may even have links or placements with a local constabulary. Occasionally there are placements offered for undergraduates on science/forensic courses at the Forensic Science Service.

What Else

As you might expect, a strong stomach and an ability to cope well in unpleasant situations is vital. You will also need to work well with other legal and police teams.

Many new entrants start as trainee forensic scientists or as reporting officers and are trained on the job over 18 months, appearing in court cases to give accurate forensics testimony. There is generally recruitment once a year for these trainee posts in summer/autumn.

The Defence Explosives Laboratory (part of the Defence Science and Technology Laboratory (DSTL)) sometimes employs forensic scientists to undertake scientific work concerning explosives.

Do not confuse the work of forensic scientists with that of scenes of crime officers, who are employed by police forces to examine the crime scene, taking fingerprints and collecting evidence (see page 58).

What It Pays

Trainee forensic scientists start on £16,000–£18,000 per year.

Prospects

This is a relatively small profession, so competition for places on specialist degree courses and for posts is intense. There may be opportunities for work abroad or in consultancies.

Best Advice

Develop your ability in chemistry and biology and attain the highest grades possible in your study. Any kind of work experience in laboratories that you can get will be useful – try a hospital pathology lab (NHS) or a school or commercial laboratory.

Contacts

The Forensic Science Service, Trident Court, 2920 Solihull Parkway, Birmingham Business Park, Birmingham B37 7 YN
0121 329 8444   www.forensic.gov.uk

DSTL
www.dstl.gov.uk

The Forensic Science Society
www.forensic-science-society.org.uk

NHS Careers
www.nhscareers.nhs.uk

Check the *New Scientist* for possible vacancies.

Geneticist

If you're considering this job, you probably know that you will be working at the cutting edge of scientific research, helping people understand how genes play a significant part in health, disease and medical abnormalities. In some ways geneticists play detective, finding out from blood, bone marrow and body fluids the exact composition of someone's particular genetic make-up so that they can help medical professionals to advise patients regarding a range of medical conditions. You may have heard of DNA analysis, but this is only a small part of the analytical work done by geneticists.

The Job Description

Most geneticists work in the NHS and are often more accurately titled cytogeneticists because they study cells (cytology) and genetics or hereditary characteristics. The types of genetic screening that geneticists undertake take place in laboratories using high-tech microscopes and computers for analysis of blood, chromosomes or fluids. They rarely come into contact with patients as their research and analysis is explained by doctors/nurses or genetic counsellors. As well as being responsible for techniques such as diagnostic testing of tissue cultures, blood chromosome analysis and sampling of amniotic fluid, their research findings can be used to treat mental and physical illnesses and even pre-natal defects.

The Person Specification

This is a highly scientific job that requires someone to be interested in the human body and the prevention and treatment of disease and ill health. You would need to be:

- fascinated by chemistry and biology
- analytical, methodical and logical
- able to record data with accuracy and attention to detail
- competent at using computers and technical equipment
- interested in assisting medical professionals with research.

What It Takes

To be a clinical cytogeneticist you will need to have a degree in biology/chemistry/biochemistry or biomedical sciences or equivalent, so you will need to have at least five GCSEs, C grades and above or equivalent, including maths, English and science plus two to three A levels/Diploma or equivalent in science subjects, particularly chemistry and biology. The NHS has a clinical scientists training scheme for graduates, leading to medical scientific careers within the health service and they look for applicants with First Class Honours or 2.i degrees. Other geneticists can work for medical research laboratories, or even forensic science services, conducting DNA tests for criminal investigations.

What Else
Geneticists can also work in agricultural research to develop bigger and better crop yields.

What It Pays
This will depend on specialism, experience and expertise, but NHS salaries start at between £23,458 and £31,779 per year.

Prospects
Consultancy to the government or genetic counselling can be other possibilities for geneticists with experience.

Best Advice
Work really hard at sciences and take an interest in anything to do with DNA, genome therapy and hereditary diseases. A work experience placement in a hospital laboratory would give you a good idea about the work – ask about working in a pathology department in the NHS.

Contacts
Association of Clinical Scientists, 130–132 Tooley Street, London SE1 2TV
020 7940 8960   www.assclinsci.org

NHS Recruitment Centre for Clinical Scientists
www.nhsclinicalscientist.info

NHS Careers
www.nhscareers.nhs.uk

Golf Greenkeeper

Golf greenkeepers are responsible for the maintenance and repair of golf courses. They are experts in everything to do with sports turf, which is something of a science these days. Greenkeepers help in the construction of new golf courses, including the technical side of green and fairway maintenance. Their role is crucial in ensuring that golf courses are playable, regardless of weather conditions, for as much of the year as is possible.

The Job Description
Greenkeepers are involved in every stage of the golf course maintenance process, from the construction of greens and bunkers, including tree maintenance, to mowing and treating the grass to develop the perfect playing conditions. It can mean something as simple as brushing the dew off greens in the morning, through to the construction of new bunkers or holes. It involves irrigation of greens and fairways, raking of sand bunkers, weed and pest control and the application of fertilisers. Greenkeepers also have to deal with re-turfing of greens, tree planting and drainage problems. Essentially, they are the horticultural expert on the golf course and have the power to close the course if they think play will have a detrimental effect.

The Person Specification
You would need to have an interest in an outdoor job and, preferably, in golf. You would need to be:

- physically fit, as you would have to walk long distances
- interested in plants, trees and maintaining the landscape
- able to work with different kinds of horticultural machinery
- able to deal with dangerous chemicals and fertilisers in a safe and responsible way
- an outdoor type of person who would not mind adverse weather conditions.

What It Takes
It is possible to gain an apprenticeship with a golf club to train for golf greenkeeping and take NVQs to Level 2 in Sports Turf and Level 3 in Sports Turf Maintenance. Other people train through a horticulturally based training course at a college and then seek employment. These courses may be NVQ courses or National Certificate/Diploma courses in sports turf. There are even Foundation degrees in sports turf and Honours degrees in turfgrass science which would lead into higher-level technical jobs at major golf clubs or for golf course design consultancies.

Many students on college or university courses have the chance to tend the turf at Twickenham or Old Trafford; they even have work placements on American golf courses as part of the training. Completion of these courses is accepted for registration as a greenkeeper and higher level courses can lead to golf course management. You could even find yourself hosting The Open Championship one day.

What Else

As mentioned before, this job is becoming more technical and involves considerably more than mowing the grass, so good training is recommended. There is also a Master Greenkeepers' Certificate which is available through the British and International Golf Greenkeepers' Association (BIGGA) and is highly regarded in the industry.

It is likely that you will need to take certificates of competence in the safe use of pesticides and general health and safety as well as acquiring the qualifications above.

What It Pays

Pay scales start at about £150–£250 per week for greenkeepers, depending on experience, qualifications and size of club.

Prospects

For those with recognised qualifications and experience, job prospects are good, with possibilities for travel abroad. Some greenkeepers take further NVQs at Level 4 in Golf Supervisory Management and with experience can move on to head greenkeeper posts and eventually golf course management/course design.

Best Advice

The website for BIGGA has excellent help and advice about this career.

Contacts

British International Golf Greenkeepers' Association (BIGGA), Bigga House, Aldwark, Alne, York YO61 1UF
01347 833800   www.bigga.co.uk

A list of accredited greenkeeping courses can be found on the Greenkeepers Training Committee website www.the-gtc.co.uk/careers.

Greetings Card Designer/ Versewriter/Poet

These careers are related but not terribly similar. Nonetheless they are worth connecting simply because the greetings card companies are the common employers for both jobs. You probably realise that greetings cards are big business, but you may not know how much work goes into their production. The range and variety of everyday and seasonal cards available in specialist shops, large supermarkets, department stores, stationers, on the internet and through booksellers is proof of the scope of the greetings card industry. Nonetheless, it is a hugely competitive market, so designs and verses become crucial to the successful marketing of greetings card ranges.

The Job Descriptions

Designers work through the whole design process, from the first concept to the final artwork stage. Their role can involve illustration, use of digital photography, mocking-up skills including the use of desktop publishing software, reprographics and print and even packaging design.

Poets or **copywriters** supply rhyming verses or comic couplets, reflecting the theme of the card. They may have to coordinate with designers to fit in with themes or they may just come up with hundreds of witty lines, emotional greetings or specialist verses for a range of seasonal and everyday situations.

The Person Specification

Designers have to have excellent drawing and visualising skills and be genuinely creative. You would need to be:

- flexible and enthusiastic
- able to work in a variety of styles and media
- computer literate, particularly with design packages, preferably with Apple Mac, QuarkXPress and Adobe Photoshop/Illustrator packages
- able to work from an initial concept and focus on the detail
- able to work to deadlines
- organised and meticulous.

Poets/copywriters/versewriters have to be immensely creative and innovative. You would have to be:

- an excellent communicator
- able to spark off ideas for different occasions
- able to write compelling, moving or witty verses that may or may not rhyme

- able to work to deadlines
- able to work on your own or in a team.

What It Takes

Designers will probably have studied a visual design/graphics/illustration degree, which may have included a work placement or sandwich year in industry or a design studio of some kind. Job adverts often require a minimum of two years' experience in a studio environment because this develops the real-world skills and ability to work under pressure that degree courses may not provide.

Poets/copywriters/versewriters may have studied a variety of different courses such as English, advertising, creative writing or even journalism. But essentially they secure work by showing examples of their writing or copy, so anyone who has the skill to do this could gain work.

What Else

Designers may work in-house for a greetings card company or on a freelance basis for several companies.

Poets often work on a freelance basis for various companies, although there may be copywriting posts in-house as well, for successful and productive writers of verse/lines.

What It Pays

This is difficult to gauge, but in-house designers may start on approximately £13,000–£17,000 per year. Experienced and trusted freelancers can earn £40 per hour. Verse writers are paid according to the type and length of verse.

Prospects

This is a competitive field, especially for freelance work where it can be difficult to establish a reputation. Freelance designers or poets have to continually market their work by presenting examples of their portfolio to companies, so business and promotion skills can be as important as creativity. Check the Hallmark and Watermark Publishing websites to see vacancies.

Best Advice

Any kind of work experience in a greetings card company would be useful.

D&AD have a graduate placement scheme which offers design opportunities for the best design graduates – they link star design graduates up with design companies.

Research the market by checking out retail and internet card companies. Find out where your writing or design style would most fit. Use business directories available at local libraries to identify greetings card companies in your area. Phone up companies and ask for their advice as to the best way to make a start in this industry and research suitable university courses that will give you the skills and placement experience to develop your potential.

Contacts

The Chartered Society of Designers, 1 Cedar Court, Royal Oak Yard, Bermondsey Street, London SE1 3GA
020 7357 8088   www.csd.org.uk

Design Week
www.designweek.co.uk

D&AD
www.dandad.org

Hallmark
www.hallmarkuk.com

Watermark Publishing
www.watermarkpublishing.com

Health Education/
Health Promotion Officer

Health education or promotion officers work in education, training and publicity for initiatives to promote good health in the population. If you think of anti-smoking, drugs education or healthy eating programmes that have been promoted through the media, then these were all part of government health services or charity campaigns. Health education involves the analysis of existing health policies and the delivery of effective health promotion initiatives in any number of ways, through publicity materials, TV campaigns, talks, presentations, research projects and community work.

The Job Description
The work can be at various levels including the planning and implementation of new government health policies, disease prevention and educational initiatives, work for hospitals in the re-education of patients and for specific charities for cancer research or heart disease prevention. A health promotion officer could be delivering talks in schools and colleges on sexual health, or working for a well-woman group, or conducting research for a health authority.

The Person Specification
Health educators are on a mission to improve the health of the planet, so they usually prefer to be involved in the prevention of illness and disease rather than the after-effects. They have to be fascinated with health and health education and want to explore different approaches to improving the overall well-being of the population. They have to be prepared to develop the skills and knowledge to challenge perceptions of health and to become effective and compelling communicators on this subject. You would need to be:

- able to analyse scientific and health data and make sense of it
- good at coming up with new ideas or ways of promoting health initiatives
- an excellent communicator, both in writing and verbally
- committed to health education as a concept.

What It Takes
This is often a second career progression for nurses, health visitors, teachers or social workers and normally a degree in biological, social or behavioural sciences is needed. In addition, a professional nursing, social work or teaching qualification is often required. There are some

specialised degree courses in health studies with health promotion at various universities, so check individual university prospectuses. Normally A levels/Diploma or equivalent in subjects like biology or human physiology or sociology or psychology are required for entry to courses, along with a good GCSE profile (C grades and over) or equivalent.

What Else
Many health educators have taken Postgraduate Diplomas in health education and promotion after experience in nursing or social work. This type of qualification can be taken through an in-service route, while working for the NHS.

What It Pays
Salaries can be in the region of £18,000–£25,000 per year to start with. Pay for experienced staff ranges from £20,000–£30,000 per year on average.

Prospects
Health is a key issue in people's lives, so career opportunities in this area, particularly in research projects and campaigns to educate people about the causes of ill-health, are increasing. Other opportunities with Sure Start centres and even the World Health Organization are available.

Best Advice
Research this carefully and start paying attention to health education campaigns. Start reading the *Health Service Journal*.

Contacts
Department of Health (DH), Quarry House, Quarry Hill, Leeds LS2 7UE
0113 254 5000   www.dh.gov.uk

NHS Careers
www.nhscareers.nhs.uk

Health Development Agency
www.hda-online.org.uk

World Health Organization
www.who.int

Sure Start
www.surestart.gov.uk

Health Informatics Officer

Health informatics is a scientific field within medicine that collects and shares biomedical information to help doctors and medical professionals make good decisions and recommendations. The growth of health informatics and its emerging importance is a result of rapid advances in technology and the growing belief that good diagnosis of medical conditions should come from evidence-based research which can also inform future treatments.

The Job Description

Clinical decisions have to be made all the time and data is being created all over the world. Health informatics professionals ensure that this information is recorded, disseminated and shared through articles in medical journals and via the internet. A health informatics officer has a responsibility to design and deliver computer systems, procedures, programmes and software to ensure that the results of research projects or medical trials can be properly shared with medical professionals in similar or related fields. The information provided is used as a key clinical tool in diagnosis and treatment so that patients can be more confident about suggested treatments and any possible side effects. It may also support the prevention of ill health and the promotion of strategies to ensure good health.

The Person Specification

The job itself requires an interest in medicine and health along with high-level expertise in computing and the management of complex data; you would have to be committed to providing information systems and data collection to support critical medical care. You would need to be:

- interested in health and medicine
- good with computers and prepared to study computing at a high level, in particular for the design and use of databases
- prepared to pay attention to detail
- methodical, logical and accurate in recording data.

What It Takes

You may choose to gain a high level of expertise in computing with at least a Foundation degree or Honours degree in information technology/database design and/or computing. There is also a specialist Honours degree in Biomedical Informatics offered by St George's Medical School at the University of London. For this route, you will need to gain at least four GCSEs, C grade and above or equivalent, and at least two A levels/Diploma or equivalent, including IT or computing. As this involves

statistical work, maths or statistics A level could also be useful.
It may be valuable, of course, to have a biological subject as well.

Alternatively, you could gain a health records administrative role in the
NHS with just four GCSEs C grade and over or equivalent. Once in this
role you may be able to undertake in-service training for advanced level
or Level 3 qualifications which would allow you to take a Foundation
degree in health informatics (such as the one offered by the University
of Central Lancashire www.uclan.ac.uk). Some universities with strong
medical and computing departments may offer the chance of project work
on medical data, which would be good experience for health informatics.

What Else
This is a growing area of work with career opportunities available in
NHS trusts, pharmaceutical companies and medical research councils.
For higher-paid and more specialist roles, postgraduate study in health
informatics will be necessary.

What It Pays
NHS salary bands start at £16,000, progressing to £31,000 per year.

Prospects
This is a relatively new profession with career opportunities throughout
the UK and overseas.

Best Advice
Work hard at maths and sciences and IT. Try some work experience in the
medical records area of your local hospital.

Contacts
NHS Careers
www.nhscareers.nhs.uk

British Health Informatics Society
www.bhis.org

Hypnotherapist

You might imagine that this job is slightly mysterious and strange when, in fact, it is a recognised part of therapy that can help people find ways to overcome personal problems, phobias, addictive behaviour or depression. Hypnotherapists are quite different in their approach to the TV or stage hypnotists you may have seen, although they may use some of the same skills or techniques. If you can remember having a relaxing daydream, then that feeling is very close to the trance state that a hypnotherapist encourages in a client. By allowing and helping a client or patient to go into a trance, the hypnotherapist can encourage a person to discover the deeper reasons for a phobia or overeating or smoking, the awareness of which can help someone overcome these problems if they truly want to.

The Job Description

Most hypnotherapists will see their clients individually, and at an initial consultation will explain the value of hypnosis and take details of the presenting problem, which normally has a subconscious cause. For example, someone might have a panic attack at the sight of a lift without knowing why this should be the case.

The hypnotherapist will introduce the client to a trance state by using a particular sequence of words and phrases and a particular tone of voice. Within this state, the hypnotherapist might make particular suggestions, which will be taken in by the subconscious mind, to help overcome the problem. This type of therapy is based on sound psychological principles and there are strict rules about how hypnotherapists must practise. The client may come for a number of sessions to work on a particular problem and may be given set tasks to do in the weeks between meetings to reinforce their own capability to deal with the problem.

The Person Specification

Hypnotherapists have to be very interested in the mind and how it works and how problems can pop up in people's lives. They must be professional and extremely ethical. You would need to be:

- caring and a good listener
- interested in psychology
- prepared to learn and practise the techniques that induce a relaxed trance state
- mature and calm with the ability to change your voice tone and pitch
- willing to take specialist training and study.

What It Takes

Many hypnotherapists have trained in psychotherapy, or have taken counselling courses, and use hypnotherapy as an additional skill. You would probably need at least some A levels/Diploma or equivalent, and possibly a degree, before you could start hypnotherapy training with the recognised professional bodies. Specifically A levels/Diploma or equivalent and/or a degree in psychology could be useful, and counselling qualifications at an advanced level would be valuable. There is a course at the University of Central Lancashire called Counselling and Psychotherapy which is the kind of course that would offer a good grounding for further training.

There are a number of routes to training – for example someone might take a psychology degree then follow this with a postgraduate psychotherapy course of training which would include hypnotherapy. Another person might take counselling qualifications for four years to Advanced Diploma level (through part-time study at a college) and then progress to a psychotherapy or hypnotherapy course. It is worth researching different ways to train through the contacts section below.

What Else

Hypnotherapy training is generally offered through private schools and colleges and can, therefore, be expensive. Some doctors and dentists take medical hypnotism courses to offer pain relief or to suppress irritating or stress-related symptoms.

What It Pays

Most hypnotherapists are self-employed and may charge between £30 and £100 per hour.

Prospects

Hypnotherapy can be used within other careers in the health service, in stress management and in cancer care.

Best Advice

Read about the mind, the unconscious and hypnosis. Take courses in psychology and counselling. Check the accredited courses recommended by the Hypnotherapy Society and the British Association of Counselling and Psychotherapy.

Contacts

The Hypnotherapy Society, Room 111, Bridge House, Bridge Street, Taunton TA1 1TD
0870 850 3387   www.hynotherapysociety.com

British Association of Counselling and Psychotherapy (BACP)
www.bacp.co.uk

Intelligence Officer/Analyst

Most people think of police work as just the visible work of policemen/women and detectives, a mix of images from various police TV programmes; but every constabulary or police authority employs civilian analysts to manage and make sense of the huge amounts of information that come in on a regular basis. Instead of just reacting to crime, intelligence analysts are part of the process of preventing and predicting criminal activity and protecting the public by reducing potential criminal behaviour. Analysts might work for police services or government security departments such as MI5 and the work generally involves in-depth research into the workings of organised crime or terrorism and assessment of information to assist the police or the government in this complex and vital work.

The Job Description

Typically, analysts receive information, which may or may not be accurate or reliable, from a wide range of sources. They have to identify patterns of activity or behaviour and make reasonable assessments of what particular information or data could mean. Through their analysis and checking of data they support security services in deciding the best way to tackle crime, terrorism or threats to citizens. They have to use thorough and detailed research methods to develop intelligence from all kinds of sources, including databases and sensitive data, which help them to make recommendations or write detailed reports which might be seen by government ministers or police investigators. Their assessments and reports inform the work of the law enforcement officers. Their swift and accurate analysis of data allows police to move quickly in investigations and surveillance.

The Person Specification

Analysts need to be knowledgeable enough to analyse intelligence (information received) and make accurate deductions about its usefulness. They have to be confident enough of their findings to enable them to produce well-researched reports for police or security service use, based on analysis of crime reports, witness statements or through compiling victim/suspect profiles. They have to be prepared to trawl through seemingly boring or incomplete data, always ready to pick out what might be important and relevant. For this work you would need to be:

- able to pay attention to detail and select what is relevant from what might be incomplete data
- able to develop a hypothesis (your understanding of the possible meaning of the data) based on clear evidence

- a good communicator who is able to give briefings in person or by detailed reports to police officers/security personnel in a concise way
- mathematical/analytical and able to work quickly and accurately with a thoroughly logical approach
- able to use computers for research and for complex testing of data
- able to work in a team, on your own initiative and to deadlines
- a person of integrity with strong values and commitment to crime prevention and national security.

What It Takes

Most jobs when advertised ask for at least five GCSEs or equivalent with C grades and above including English and maths, and two A levels/ Diploma or equivalent. A degree in criminology or a maths/science is probably an advantage and is essential for MI5/MI6 work. Selection tests for these roles often assess maths ability and personality qualities such as determination and personal integrity. Training is offered within the job – particularly in using specialist computer software.

What Else

The main employers will be police services or security service government departments. The Official Secrets Act will probably apply to the work so you may not be able to divulge to your friends or family what you do. You will probably be background checked before being offered a contract.

What It Pays

Starting salaries for analysts are in the range of £21,000–£25,000 per year but experienced analysts earn £27,000–£35,000 and upwards depending on the complexity of the work undertaken.

Prospects

Analysts work mainly for individual constabularies, the Metropolitan Police, the Serious Organised Crime Agency (SOCA), the National Policing Improvement Agency (NPIA), MI5 (inland security) or MI6 (worldwide security).

Best Advice

There is plenty of useful information on the job roles within intelligence work on the MI5/MI6, SOCA and NPIA websites. You can also look out for vacancies advertised by your local or regional constabulary.

Contacts

NPIA
020 7147 8200   www.npia.police.uk

SOCA
www.soca.gov.uk

MI5
www.mi5.gov.uk

MI6
www.mi6.gov.uk

Metropolitan Police
www.metpolicecareers.co.uk/intelligence

Interior Designer

It is easy to be attracted to this kind of work at a time when interest in innovative house-design projects is so popular, but it is important to realise that, despite all this publicity, job opportunities in interior design are fairly limited. However, for creative people with an interest in using a variety of artistic media, this can be the perfect career.

Interior designers are responsible for the total design of the interiors of buildings, houses, pubs, hotels, department stores and even cruise liners and aircraft. They advise their clients on the whole interior look, including furniture, fabrics, window effects, fixtures and fittings, lighting, paint colours and effects, and decoration.

The Job Description

Interior designers plan and supervise the design of interiors, working with architects and construction professionals to ensure that the living or working space is usefully organised and attractively planned. They have to creatively plan the best use of the space and to come up with design ideas for the interior. The work involves a range of expertise, using artistic talent, drawing skills including computer-aided design, knowledge of textiles and floor coverings, an eye for colour and lighting, and an ability to prepare cost estimates that fit the client's budget.

The Person Specification

Designers have to prepare working drawings after initial consultation with the client, which may be freehand drawings or computer designs. They use their knowledge of the theory of design, architecture, colour and lighting effects to create attractive and practical designs. They have to inspect the work as it is under way, and supervise and liaise with those who are doing the work. You would need to be:

- creative and full of design ideas
- able to come up with practical solutions to design problems
- willing to present ideas and designs to a client and change them, where necessary, according to the client's ideas or budget
- good at 3D design with an eye for colour
- confident when dealing with customers
- computer literate, especially using design packages
- able to work to deadlines and coordinate a project with many different skilled workers.

What It Takes

Most interior designers have a degree in interior design or spatial/3D design. Normal entry qualifications for these courses are 2–3 A levels/ Diploma or equivalent including an art or design subject, a BTEC National Diploma or Certificate in a design subject, or an art Foundation course, together with a portfolio of design ideas. Talented designers with an excellent portfolio may gain a place on higher level courses without the usual academic requirements.

There are also some one- and two-year interior design courses that are run by colleges (often BTEC diplomas) and which may be enough to gain work; however, due to competition for jobs, it may be advisable to take a higher level university course.

What Else

Designers often work on a self-employed or consultancy basis, in partnership with architectural firms or as an in-house designer for hotel and retail chains.

What It Pays

Typical starting salaries are around £15,000–£20,000 per year. Higher earnings are possible for experienced designers and freelancers decide their own rates.

Prospects

Other areas of career progression can be in exhibition and theatre design. Freelance work is very common. Some house-building companies employ designs on a freelance basis for showhouse design and decoration.

Best Advice

Train your eye by visiting museums, stately homes and galleries. Research architectural styles and learn paint and stencilling techniques. Start a design book where you cut out ideas from magazines and collect paint charts from decorating stores. Start designing different types of rooms and save good ideas for your portfolio. The British Interior Design Association offers good advice and a list of degree and short courses.

Contacts

The British Interior Design Association (BIDA), 3–18 Chelsea Harbour Design Centre, Lots Road, London SW10 0XE
020 7349 0800   www.bida.org

Jockey

There is quite a bit more to being a jockey than loving horses, but jockeys spend so much of their time with them that a passion for all things equine is a good starting point. Jockeys and stable lads (unisex term) are responsible for the basic exercising and grooming of horses. Following this experience, jockeys get the chance to ride horses in flat races (flat jockey) or for National Hunt races (involving jumps – jump jockey) for the racehorse's owner.

The Job Description

Jockeys are outside in all weathers, working long, unsocial hours. Initially the work, as stable staff, will include mucking-out, sweeping, feeding, grooming, exercising and caring for the horses. To be eligible to ride in races, jockeys have to be committed to keeping their weight down, which involves careful attention to diet and fitness. Getting rides for racehorse owners and trainers is reliant on weight and performance, so this is a somewhat pressurised existence. Most jockeys start off as a stable lad, in the hope of being offered an apprentice or 'conditional' jockey training at a later stage. Apprentice jockeys become flat-racing jockeys; conditional apprentices become jump jockeys (National Hunt). Competition for jockey training is intense.

The Person Specification

Jockeys need to be confident riders and need good physical fitness and courage for when controlling a spirited horse. They have to be able to work out/plan the best race strategy for their horse. They need good basic educational skills in English and maths, and, most importantly, a real love of horses and a competitive outlook. You will need to be:

- ideally under eight stone in weight for flat racing and under nine-and-a-half stone for jump racing
- able to pass a stringent medical
- patient, when dealing with horses
- able to react quickly and have good eyesight
- a confident and keen rider
- prepared to be outside in all weathers and working for long hours.

What It Takes

NVQs Levels 1 and 2 in Racehorse Care can be taken by new trainees employed by stables. Racing schools at Newmarket and Doncaster offer initial residential training courses of 9–12 weeks for stable staff and then exceptional applicants may be offered apprenticeships. Apprenticeships last a further two years and then, if competent, the jockey applies for a licence to ride with a licensed trainer.

What Else

Interestingly, racing schools do not always insist that trainees have riding experience and will consider interested applicants who suit the weight and size restrictions even if this is lacking.

Jockeys' careers can be seriously affected if they grow too big or put on weight.

What It Pays

Pay rates for stable staff are generally in the region of £170–£189 per week plus accommodation. Experienced jockeys are paid a fee per ride and a percentage of any winnings.

Prospects

Competition is tough at jockey level. Alternative careers related to this work might be as head lad, travelling head lad or as assistant trainer – see the British Horseracing Board site for further information.

Best Advice

Check the British Horseracing Board website for more details about a range of careers in the horseracing industry.

Contacts

British Horseracing Board, 151 Shaftesbury Avenue, London WC2H 8AL
020 7152 0000   www.careersinracing.com

British Racing School, Newmarket
www.brs.org.uk

Northern Racing College, Doncaster
www.northernracingcollege.co.uk

Lexicographer

You've probably used some kind of dictionary before – it might have been a basic English dictionary or a dual-language dictionary which helped you work out how to make sense of a restaurant menu when you were on holiday. Lexicographers are the people who create and compile dictionaries, which are used every day by millions of people. It may seem mindboggling to think that someone records all the uses, exact definitions and examples of each and every word. However, lexicographers are fascinated by language and get a buzz from ensuring that their dictionaries are as complete as possible, and that new words circulating in specialist or everyday contexts are featured and defined as appropriate.

The Job Description

Lexicographers are responsible for the creation and updating of dictionaries, deciding which words will be included. They check meanings of general and specialist words and find ways to describe a word as concisely as possible. They keep a check on new words as they gain popularity, whether through newspapers, TV or in literature, and decide whether they need to be introduced into dictionaries, determining the best definitions, assigning specific meanings to a new word or even a phrase. For language dictionaries, they will need to know how to translate a word from one language to another and be confident that the detailed definition they offer makes perfect sense to a speaker of another language.

The Person Specification

This is a job for someone who is passionate about language, grammar and the derivations of words. You would need to be extremely aware of words and have a broad vocabulary with a curiosity for new or unusual words. You would need to be:

- meticulous and organised
- accurate, with great attention to detail
- able to focus and notice errors
- confident with English and possibly another foreign language
- a grammar expert
- confident using computers, particularly databases.

What It Takes

Most lexicographers work for specialist dictionary publishers and train on the job. Most start as graduate trainees after a degree in a subject such as English, linguistics, classics or a foreign language. You will need a good GCSE profile, C grades and over or equivalent including English, maths, science and probably a foreign language, and A levels/Diploma to gain a place on a degree course. For foreign-language dictionaries, a foreign-language degree, which would include a year abroad, will be essential, followed perhaps by a translating studies postgraduate course. Many trainee lexicographers study at postgraduate or Master's level to gain additional skills and experience – the MA in Language and Lexicography at Birmingham University Dictionary Research Centre might help someone gain a graduate traineeship with a specialist dictionary publisher. The course includes a short placement with a dictionary publisher.

What Else

This is a small profession so determination and motivation to develop the skills required will be needed. Find any way you can to develop a high standard of grammar and vocabulary.

What It Pays

Starting salaries for graduate trainees are in the region of £16,000–£18,500 per year.

Prospects

It is possible to work on a freelance basis as an editor or to move into other areas of publishing from lexicography.

Best Advice

Gain some work experience in publishing. Work hard at English and foreign languages. Scour newspapers and listen out for unusual usages or new words.

Contacts

Association for Terminology and Lexicography, 57 King Henry's Walk, London N1 4NH
www.batl.org.uk

Oxford English Dictionary
www.oed.com

Dictionary Research Centre, University of Birmingham
www.english.bham.ac.uk/DRC

Licensed Conveyancer

Every time anyone sells a property to someone else there is a legal process called conveyancing which has to be gone through. This transfers the ownership of a property into the new purchaser's name. Licensed conveyancers generally work in a solicitors' office and manage this transferral of property, including the legal documents that prove ownership.

The Job Description

Conveyancers will be instructed by a client who is in the process of purchasing a property. This may come through a bank/building society, an estate agent or through a firm of solicitors. The conveyancer will look into the legal right to own that property, conducting detailed property searches and preparing the transfer documents so that the new owner is then listed as the legal owner. This work can be done by property specialist solicitors or by licensed conveyancers.

The Person Specification

This work would suit someone with an interest in law, in particular the laws that apply to property, and with an ability to research details of ownership in a methodical way. You would need to be:

- keen to work in an administrative role
- good with clients and able to explain the details of property law in an easily understood way
- able to pay attention to detail
- accurate and logical in the way you would work
- prepared to take specialist training, accredited by the Council of Licensed Conveyancers.

What It Takes

The minimum qualifications for entry to this career are four GSCEs, C grades or above or equivalent, including English. Many applicants have A levels/Diploma or equivalent or even degrees in subjects like law, planning, surveying or business. You may need to be able to show some kind of work experience in a legal setting before being offered a place as a trainee licensed conveyancer. Once in a job as a trainee you could begin to work towards the specialist licensed conveyancer exams through the Council for Licensed Conveyancers (CLC), which can be taken by distance learning or through specialist colleges. Once you have passed these exams, you would train for a further two years under the supervision of a qualified conveyancer or solicitor.

If you take a degree in law or have taken legal executive qualifications through the Institute of Legal Executives (ILEX), you may be exempt from some of the CLC exams.

What Else

It is possible to take the exams after part-time/evening study or distance learning and then apply for trainee posts with legal firms. You may not see jobs advertised for trainee licensed conveyancers, so do your research and then make 'on spec' applications to firms of conveyancers or solicitors, asking about possible trainee vacancies.

What It Pays

Trainee salaries can start at about £12,000–£14,000 per year. Once trained you will earn about £14,000–£20,000 per year and higher earnings can be possible with experience.

Prospects

Self-employed or freelance work is possible as a qualified conveyancer.

Best Advice

Get some work experience in a solicitors' or surveyors' office. Try law GCSE or A level or look out for legal executive courses available at many colleges.

Contacts

Council for Licensed Conveyancers, 16 Glebe Road, Chelmsford, Essex CM1 1QG
01245 349599   www.conveyancer.org.uk

ILEX
www.ilex.org.uk

Conveyancing Jobs
www.conveyancingjobs.com

Lifestyle Adviser/Coach

Many of us want to be healthy and full of energy, and there's plenty of evidence that lifestyle changes can really make a difference. The job of a lifestyle adviser/coach is to help clients to manage their own health and lifestyles. Lifestyle advisers, sometimes referred to as coaches or even lifestyle gurus, are increasingly employed by the health service to motivate patients, particularly those at risk, such as smokers or those who are overweight or stressed.

The Job Description

Medical staff are often concerned about patients who, despite medication or even surgery, continue to suffer from a range of medical conditions which niggle away and never really get better. The causes may be complex but are often triggered by aspects of a patient's lifestyle or routine. Doctors can now refer patients to lifestyle coaches on the NHS and these advisers work with patients to address the underlying causes of their conditions, offering suggestions for changes to habits, diet and activities which could improve fitness and personal happiness. Advisers might specialise in anti-smoking coaching, weight management or general fitness/activity support.

The Person Specification

Coaches will start by discussing a patient's personal goals with them, for example, what they want to achieve and the reasons why a change of some kind is appropriate at this particular point in time. They will have detailed medical information to consider but will also do an audit of the patient's lifestyle, checking things such as their weight, height, body mass index, blood pressure and even cholesterol. They may need to ask about the patient's habits – for example, how many cigarettes do they smoke a day or how much exercise do they do a week? Having created a profile, they plan how to help the patient or client achieve their goals. They might meet them on a regular basis to support and encourage them. For this work you would need to be:

- good with people
- sensitive and empathic
- a good listener
- a good motivator
- knowledgeable about health issues and interested in health/biological sciences.

What It Takes

For most NHS posts experience of working in the health service or in health and fitness will be required. Previous work as a health-care support assistant or as a physiotherapy or dietician's assistant might lead into this work. Some jobs will require you to have fitness assessment qualifications such as those offered by the YMCA or a degree in sports science or similar. For posts in the area of nutrition or weight management a degree in nutrition might be required. For degree courses a good GCSE profile or equivalent, including English, maths and science, C grade and over plus A levels/Diploma will be needed. Advanced-level subjects such as human physiology would be particularly useful.

Personal trainer Level 3 courses, available through colleges and private fitness organisations, may also be relevant for this work as they cover cardiovascular assessment, exercise and nutrition. The YMCA qualifications in fitness and fitness assessment are also well regarded and available at colleges or through intensive courses at locations throughout the UK.

What Else

Some lifestyle coaches will work on a freelance basis or can move into magazine or media work.

What It Pays

NHS salaries start between £19,683 and £25,424 per year.

Prospects

Although the work may be mostly one-to-one coaching, advisers can do more community based and group work where they work in health-improvement teams in particular geographical areas, where poor health is a problem. Many advisers train other health-care workers and set up healthy lifestyle sessions in communities.

Best Advice

Be committed to your own health. Read books about healthy eating and lifestyle. Study psychology so that you learn to understand about motivation and behaviour change.

Contacts

The Nutrition Society, 28 Portland Place, London W1B 1DE
020 7291 8378   www.nutritionsociety.org

NHS Careers
www.nhscareers.nhs.uk

YMCAfit
www.ymcafit.org.uk

Loss Adjuster

Accidents happen. People experience minor or major disasters – it could be a tree falling through a roof, a washing machine overflowing, or something much worse. Loss adjusters work for insurance companies, investigating and checking into all kinds of situations to make sure that a claim for insurance is valid. Many claims are connected to fire, flood or damage of some kind; loss adjusters visit the site of an accident to check what has happened and verify the claim details made by the insurance customer.

The Job Description

Loss adjusters make site inspections and interview the people who are making the claim, comparing the details on the insurance claim to what they hear from talking to the claimants. They are not out to prove that the claimants are wrong, but they do need to verify that the claim is valid and not fraudulent in any way. They may resemble a police investigator in the way that they go about their job, gathering evidence, checking reports and interviewing people. Once they have approved a claim they will arrange for repair work and organise contractors who will undertake this.

The Person Specification

To do this work you would need to be able to talk to many different personalities and be sensitive to the stress caused by insurance claims. You would need to be able to analyse evidence, write reports and make recommendations in an objective way. Loss adjusters need to be particularly:

- good at communication
- analytical in their approach
- numerate and able to deal with complex calculations
- able to understand technical details
- confident and objective when dealing with claims
- interested in being fair and unbiased.

What It Takes

Most people wanting to become loss adjusters have to learn through experience from a qualified loss adjuster and take Chartered Institute of Loss Adjusters (CLA) exams at the same time. It is useful to start in an insurance company as a claims assistant, taking Chartered Insurance Institute (CII) exams and then move into trainee loss adjuster roles after experience in insurance. It is also possible to move into this work after qualifying in a range of other professions such as surveying, accountancy or building engineering, for example. Some large companies have loss adjuster graduate trainee schemes for graduates with professional degrees such as those listed above.

Claims assistants will normally need at least four GCSEs or equivalent, C grade and over, including maths and English, for most advertised jobs with insurance companies.

For degree study, you will need a good GCSE profile or equivalent, C grades and over including maths, English and science, and A levels/ Diploma in relevant subjects, according to degree subject choice.

What Else
Loss adjusters may work for a team, employed by a large insurance company or for specialist firms/consultancies. Regardless of their particular employer, they have to be professional, impartial and independent, as stipulated by the CLA.

What It Pays
Starting salaries are in the range £18,000–£24,000 per year.

Prospects
Some loss adjusters specialise in particular kinds of claims and establish a reputation for dealing with specific accidents or disasters. Others might move into areas where they investigate persistent fraud. There may be opportunities for work overseas.

Best Advice
Work hard at maths and English and develop analytical skills in any way you can. Try a work experience in an insurance company to find out how the insurance industry operates. Read articles about insurance and visit the website of Lloyd's of London – www.lloyds.com – to learn about the insurance industry from one of the most famous global insurers.

Contacts
Chartered Institute of Loss Adjusters (CLA), Warwick House, 65/66 Queen Street, London EC4R 1EB
020 7337 9960   www.cila.co.uk

Chartered Insurance Institute (CII), 42–48 High Road, South Woodford, London E18 2JP
020 8989 8464   www.cii.co.uk

Marine Biologist/Scientist

The idea of travelling and doing research work in extreme environments, such as on the sea bed or in Antarctica, might appeal to you, especially if you are fascinated by marine life and deep-sea creatures. Although it could involve diving or going underwater in a submersible, it could just as easily mean time spent in a laboratory. Marine biologists make detailed observations of marine life, gather samples and analyse data so that they can make recommendations about the protection and conservation of the marine environment, check levels of pollution and water quality and advise on the development of marine resources.

The Job Description

An exact job description of a marine biologist is fairly difficult, as there is no typical job role, but as a general rule they are involved in the study of marine plants, animals and organisms. With the world's oceans covering 71 per cent of the surface of the earth, we still know very little about many of the sea organisms, many of which might be important for our survival. Some of the uses of marine biology are as follows:

- studying the life cycles of fish might help us catch them or prevent overfishing
- certain compounds found in marine sponges might help with anti-cancer treatments
- certain marine plants can be used to check radiation levels.

Marine scientists are normally involved in collecting samples, observing organisms or processes and tagging various species (such as sharks or dolphins) to track their movements or numbers; while they may be working outdoors on a boat or diving, they may also be in a laboratory or in front of a computer.

In general, people who go into this work are tempted by the prospect of something exciting like studying whales or dolphins, but the reality of this work might find you working as a herring abundance forecaster (checking numbers of herring) or determining the environmental impact of routine developments (for the Department of Environment, Food and Rural Affairs (DEFRA), for example) due to new environmental awareness and national or international legislation.

The Person Specification

Work as a marine biologist/scientist can involve observation and data collection at sea or in a laboratory, analysis of data using computer programs such as geographical information systems (GIS), statistical surveys and the production of written reports with your findings.

While boat handling and scuba diving experience is extremely useful, you will also need to write journal articles or even present research at a scientific conference.

You will need to be highly numerate and interested in science, especially biology and conservation of the environment. You will need to be:

- accurate and pay attention to detail
- computer literate, possibly with programming skills
- analytical and good at problem solving
- able to work well in a team
- physically fit
- able, preferably, to scuba dive and handle boats.

What It Takes
Most jobs require degree-level and usually postgraduate study in biological sciences or marine biology. You would probably have to gain science A levels/Diploma or equivalent in subjects like biology, chemistry and even maths or physics.

What Else
Marine biologists often have to be prepared to travel or to apply for jobs abroad in order to develop their careers. They may find work at aquariums, universities, research labs or even on board large research ships. They may only be employed on a short-term, project-to-project basis, so work patterns can often be a little uncertain.

What It Pays
Starting salaries range from £15,000–£23,000 per year.

Prospects
Typically, marine biologists are employed by marine research laboratories, universities, government-funded organisations or even charities. Postgraduate study for additional professional and specialist qualifications is usual and may help you progress in your career, leading to management of marine projects or laboratories.

Best Advice
Gain volunteer field experience as early as possible with environmental projects or charities – check the Gap Year website for ideas: www.gapyear.com. Read *New Scientist* and *Nature* for background information and job adverts.

Contacts
The Department for Environment, Food and Rural Affairs, Nobel House, 17 Smith Square, London SW1P 3JR
08459 335577   www.defra.gov.uk

The Marine Biological Association
www.mba.ac.uk

New Scientist
www.newscientist.com

Nature Jobs
www.naturejobs.com

Mediator/Mediation Work

You might like the idea of this work if you are the kind of person who enjoys helping people solve any problems and difficulties that they may have in relation to other people. A mediator is someone who helps people who are in dispute with one another for a variety of reasons, working with them to resolve these situations.

There are different types of mediators specialising in different kinds of mediation work, such as family mediation, neighbour disputes mediation, victim–offender work, peer mediation and community mediation. Most of the people who do this work do it on a voluntary basis, but there are paid mediators throughout the UK and there are increasing opportunities for paid employment in this type of work.

The Job Description
In **family mediation**, the job involves mediating in disputes between people who are at the first stage of a divorce/separation process. Mediators are responsible for bringing the two parties together, managing the conflict and dealing with disputes. They would have to deal with the children and the family as a whole, focusing on children's rights and needs. They act as an impartial third party assisting those in dispute and help to facilitate communication in times of high conflict, aiming to avoid further distress or bitterness. They may also have to provide reports to lawyers as part of the legal process. Being able to communicate well with children and understand their rights is a key skill in family mediation.

This type of work has come about as a result of the Family Law Act and is monitored by the Legal Services Commission.

In **neighbour disputes mediation**, mediators work in a similar way to resolve disputes between neighbours, such as hostility over noise or car parking, again taking an impartial third-party role and encouraging good communication between the parties in the dispute.

Victim–offender mediation involves helping offenders become aware of the impact of their crimes by meeting a victim (with the agreement of the victim) and possibly arranging a process of making amends.

Peer mediation is a process being used in schools to combat bullying through which pupils offer support to one another to confront and deal with the situation in a positive way.

Community mediation can include victim–offender work, neighbourhood disputes, peer mediation or even broader issues such as workplace mediation concerning staff and/or manager disputes, court services mediation or complaints against the National Health Service.

The Person Specification

As a mediator, you would need to have highly developed communication skills, both verbal and written. You would need to be able to analyse complex information and be ready to deal with the strong emotions that surface in these situations.

Mediators have to be non-judgemental and aware of their own values and how these might get in the way of their work. They also need to be:

- committed to confidentiality in respect of their clients
- an outstanding communicator, with excellent listening and report-writing skills
- able to stay calm when people are expressing anger or strong emotions
- committed to arriving at an agreement that is acceptable for all parties.

What It Takes

Family mediation. No one can work as a family mediator without substantial experience and training. Family mediators ideally have at least a degree-level qualification (possibly in law, politics or social sciences) and A level/Diploma or equivalent and GCSE maths and English at C grade or equivalent.

The training for family mediation is approved by the UK College of Family Mediators and involves working as a trainee mediator under supervision, probably on a self-employed sessional basis while taking a modular part-time course lasting about eight to nine months. Once the training is completed, mediators would have to seek approval from the Legal Services Commission, before being able to work as a mediator.

Most family mediators are employed on a self-employed, sessional basis and many work part time and have a parallel career in social work or law.

Community mediation, including neighbour disputes mediation, victim–offender, peer, work-related and court services mediation work. In many areas of the country, there are various specialised volunteer training courses for community mediators. Sorting out a variety of disputes between neighbours about noise, dealing with anti-social behaviour problems or assisting in communication-breakdown situations in the community, can be an extremely valuable job.

The training is often accredited by the National Open College Network and/or by OCR (Oxford and Cambridge and RSA) – for example the OCR Diploma in Mediation Skills and Practice.

Birkbeck College, University of London also offers a Conflict Resolution and Mediation Studies Diploma – www.bbk.ac.uk.

Some volunteers move into paid jobs in this kind of mediation as funding becomes available through local councils and projects. It seems to be a growing area of jobs, so the volunteer training may be a good career move.

What Else

Paid mediators may deal with ten cases per month, typically aiming for three to five meetings to resolve a situation. Volunteers may only deal with two cases per month. However, once trained, volunteers can deal with the same types of cases as paid mediators.

Some people move into mediation work from a counselling career and counselling skills can be a useful grounding for this kind of work. Mediation training can give you transferable skills which can be used in many different careers, from social work to personnel or legal work.

This may seem an appealing career, but it does require a long period of training and substantial life experience. It can be rewarding or frustrating, depending on the outcome of the mediation.

What It Pays

Pay is often sessional, so it is difficult to give an accurate pay rate, but jobs advertised (which may be advertised as a project co-ordinator or manager including mediation work and training) show a pay range of £23,000–£25,000 per year.

Prospects

It is estimated that the number of people working as mediators is growing and so there are increasing opportunities for mediators to train other people in this work, and for freelance employment. Disruption caused by disputes at work has encouraged local authorities to develop mediation services for these personnel-related issues. Court services are also keen to employ mediators.

Best Advice

Doing some volunteer training is the best way to find out whether mediation work is for you. Contact your local county, borough or city council to find out about mediation work in your area. Basic introductory counselling courses also offer some of the skills needed for mediation.

Contacts

UK College of Family Mediators, Alexander House, Telephone Avenue, Bristol BS1 4BS
0117 904 7223   www.ukcfm.co.uk

UK Mediation
www.ukmediation.net

National Family Mediation
www.nfm.org.uk

Medical Illustrator/ Clinical Photographer

Medical illustrators/clinical photographers are responsible for the clinical recording of patient treatment through photographs, video production or artwork. Illustrative material that is produced plays a crucial part in patient care, medical education and research. By recording medical conditions in a visual way, illustrators can help medical professionals assess the progress of an illness, assist with teaching medical students to recognise different medical conditions and contribute to on-going medical research. If you have ever looked at pictures of medical conditions or diseases in a medical encyclopaedia, then you have seen the work of a medical illustrator.

The Job Description

Within the NHS, medical illustrators provide essential photographic services to medical and paramedical staff, which can help in early diagnosis or confirmation of illnesses or disease. The visual records of patients' conditions they create allow doctors, dentists and medical students to monitor and treat a range of health conditions. They use a variety of specialised techniques such as ultra-violet and infra-red photography and graphic service. They are responsible for the production of audio-visual materials for teaching, and artwork for medical posters and publications. They could be working in a studio, an operating theatre, a ward or a clinic. In an operating department, medical photographers may illustrate the stages of a new surgical technique, for use by students.

The Person Specification

An illustrator has to have a combination of many skills, including technical expertise, an understanding of physiology and anatomy, drawing skills and a caring, sympathetic approach to patients. Illustrators can specialise in the photographic/video side or the graphics/artistic side. You will need to be:

- friendly, sympathetic and professional
- good at working as part of a team
- artistic
- familiar with basic anatomy
- able to use your initiative
- painstaking in attention to detail
- able to remain detached when photographing unpleasant skin conditions or diseases.

What It Takes

To join the profession of medical illustrators as a student member, you will need to have a degree or HND/Foundation degree qualification in visual media, such as photography, graphics or video production. It is possible to study a degree course on a full-time basis, specialising in clinical photography at the University of Westminster, which involves a work placement in a clinical setting. To gain access to art-based media/photography courses you would probably need a portfolio of artwork, A levels or a BTEC National Diploma in an art or photographic subject and possibly an art Foundation qualification. For the University of Westminster course, the entry requirements are A level/Diploma qualifications in maths, physics, chemistry, biology or photography, or a combination of these subjects.

What Else

Most student medical illustrators aim to be qualified through CAMIP (Committee for Accreditation of Medical Illustration Practitioners) courses via part time/full time or postgraduate qualifications in clinical photography – check the IMI (Institute of Medical Illustrators) website for information about the range of suitable courses.

What It Pays

NHS pay rates for illustrators show starting salaries of £14,037 per year, rising to £31,000 per year for those with experience and CAMIP qualifications.

Prospects

There are further training courses available through the Institute of Medical Illustrators which can help improve members' career prospects.

Best Advice

Check out the Institute's website for examples of medical illustrators' work.

Contacts

Institute of Medical Illustrators, 29 Arboretum Street, Nottingham NG1 4JA
www.imi.org.uk

CAMIP
www.camip.org.uk

University of Westminster
www.westminster.ac.uk

Mudlogger

This sounds like the ideal job for a small child who likes grubbing around in the mud. In fact, this is a highly technical job within an oil company, working on an oil-drilling rig. Mudloggers are responsible for collecting geological samples, which can prove the presence of oil or gas, and checking and monitoring the whole drilling process.

The Job Description
Using highly technical equipment and binocular microscopes, mudloggers work in specialist laboratories on rigs, checking computer recordings of drillings, analysing samples and reporting information back to the oil company. They are there to ensure the success of the drilling operation as well as being responsible for elements of the centrally important safety processes.

The Person Specification
Work on oil rigs can be dangerous, noisy and can, typically, involve long 12-hour days and shift patterns. The person suited to this work would need to like being in different locations for each contract, working with many different types of people in a quite intense atmosphere and be interested in science/technology. You would need to be:

- interested in geography/geology
- analytical and methodical
- good with computers and strongly mathematical
- keen to work in a laboratory environment (possibly on a rig in the middle of the sea)
- happy about being away from home for long periods.

What It Takes
Most companies that employ mudloggers expect applicants to have degrees, or possibly HNDs, in chemistry, mining engineering, geophysics/geology or physics. You would need GCSEs at C grade and above, or equivalent, in maths, English and science, and A levels/Diploma for entry to university courses.

What Else
All employees new to oil/extraction companies will go through induction training in data collection, safety and survival. Health and safety awareness is paramount on oil rigs.

What It Pays
Starting salaries range from £20,000–£25,000 per year.

Prospects

There are prospects for career moves into other areas of drilling operations and work with oil companies around the world.

Best Advice

Work experience with oil companies or civil engineering companies is valuable. Any laboratory experience would also be useful.

Contacts

Geological Society of London, Burlington House, Piccadilly, London W1V 0JU
020 7434 9944   www.geolsoc.org

Society of Exploration Geophysicists
www.seg.org

Earthworks
www.earthworks-jobs.com

Music Journalist

If you're mad about music and love to read the specialist music magazines or listen to music reviews on the radio, this job might really interest you. It combines two big areas of expertise – knowing a lot about a particular type of music, such as classical, jazz or rock and pop, and being able to communicate that enthusiasm in written form, through articles or reviews.

The Job Description

Working for a music magazine, newspaper or radio station, you will be promoting or criticising particular types of music. You will have to have a passion for music and will probably be listening to it constantly. That is the easy bit. You must also be able to write about music in a witty and fluent way. The writing skills are, if anything, more important than the musical knowledge. As this is a very competitive and restricted line of work (there are only so many jobs and loads of people chasing them), you would need to develop an individual and lucid writing style, as well as an in-depth knowledge of music.

The Person Specification

Music journalists have to be good at research, keen to extend their own music preferences, constantly on the search for new sounds/performers/ bands and good at networking/making new contacts in the music industry. They might also have to withstand the persuasion of promotions departments of big music companies who might offer incentives to feature their bands. You would need to be:

- good at writing
- able to interview musicians for stories
- passionate and knowledgeable about a particular type of music
- organised and good at research with a good ear for new sounds.

What It Takes

The normal way to train for this is through a journalism course after A levels/Diploma. The National Council for the Training of Journalists (NCTJ) and the Periodicals Training Council (PTC) list accredited courses – these are the ones to go for. There are some universities that allow you to combine a journalism course with a minor course in music. It may be possible to study a music or music technology course and follow this with a postgraduate journalism course.

The London College of Communication at the University of the Arts, London offers some useful short courses in magazine journalism which might just give you the edge – www.lcc.arts.ac.uk.

The hardest part will be to get your first job as a music journalist, so you will have to prove that you can write in a truly zappy way and bombard editors with ideas for articles, offering examples of your writing.

What Else

Offer to work for free for a fan club of your favourite band – get some articles written and send them through to fan magazines.

What It Pays

Starting salaries range from £18,000–£24,000 per year but increasingly the majority of magazine journalists are freelancers, meaning that pay rates are variable. Check the Society for Editors and Proofreaders' website (www.sfep.org.uk) for an idea of minimum rates. The National Union of Journalists also offers advice on this. As a broad rule, many freelancers are paid around £200 for 1,000 words of writing.

Prospects

Music journalists move into radio and TV jobs or public relations work with music companies.

Best Advice

Go to as many concerts as you can and offer to do promotions for any local bands. Write press releases and send them to local newspapers. Keep evidence of any that get published. Start a music blog on the internet and aim to write something every day. Check out music sites such as www.slicethepie.com, where you can pick up experience and get paid for it as a music scout/reviewer of new bands.

Contacts

The National Council for the Training of Journalists (NCTJ), The New Granary, Station Road, Newport, Saffron Walden, Essex CB11 3PL
01799 544014   www.nctj.com

PTC (Periodicals Training Council)
www.ppa.co.uk

National Union of Journalists
www.nuj.org.uk

NME (New Musical Express)
www.nme.com

Mystery Shopper

This job sounds a dream job for someone who likes shopping and wants a job with an interesting title. It has been created by the need for companies, in particular retailers, hotels and restaurants, to know what their customers think of the service they receive. Using a mystery shopper is a way of checking out what customers really want and helps companies prevent customer/staff miscommunication by making use of this confidential/anonymous feedback.

The Job Description

Retailers, hotels and restaurants, banks and building societies, colleges and universities, to name but a few, really need to canvass their customers' views on services they are offering. These types of service organisations have to know that they have got things right and that their staff are offering a consistent service. A mystery shopper is employed by an independent organisation to go into a service organisation to test it out. They may be an average shopper, making a simple purchase, but, unknown to the shop assistant, they will be assessing the assistant for courtesy, helpfulness, etc. They may have to act as a difficult customer, demanding an exchange to determine how well the service works in a challenging situation. They may book a table at a restaurant and assess the food and service provided. They may contact a bank for financial advice and, using pre-set questions, compare the service to the bank's competitors.

Organisations that use mystery shopper services are keen to gain feedback on their services and will agree scenarios that need to be tested and questions that have to be asked. As you can see, it is not just about having fun shopping.

The Person Specification

Many mystery shoppers do this work on a part-time basis or as a student job. It is good experience for marketing or advertising careers. In some cases, the mystery shopper will act like a normal customer, and will never reveal their real identity or purpose. They may have to do some secret filming while in the store or restaurant, for example. You would need to be:

- good at role playing
- a good communicator
- flexible, adaptable and accurate
- quick thinking
- good at assessing services.

Often a mystery shopper may have to complete a survey on aspects such as premises, cleanliness, staff friendliness, product quality, and access for the disabled. This may involve careful but discreet record keeping and the production of a written report within 24 hours of a visit.

What It Takes
No specific qualifications are demanded, but a good education and an ability to relate well to a wide range of people is necessary.

What Else
Most mystery shoppers work for specialist agencies who may be involved in other market research. Increasingly as well as 'field' mystery shoppers who go out on visits, organisations are using telephone mystery shoppers, based in an office or at home, who make calls to organisations to test out their services.

What It Pays
Average pay rates can be about £5–£10 per individual assignment. This is rarely a full-time job but can provide a supplementary income.

Prospects
This could lead into careers in market research, marketing, advertising or customer service training.

Best Advice
Try this work out on a temporary basis to see if it suits you. Good mystery shopper agencies will ask you to register your details and then you may have initial training followed by your first assignment.

Contacts
Contact market research agencies and check on the internet where many mystery shopper vacancies are advertised.

Naval Architect

If you have ever found yourself interested in the design and construction of ships, boats, warships, submarines, yachts and even offshore drilling platforms, then you might like to consider training as a naval architect. A naval architect can be involved in the engineering design of these large structures, including their actual construction, their repair or renovation, overseeing the project and consultancy to shipbuilders or the maritime industry.

The Job Description

This is essentially a professional engineering activity with the naval architect leading a team of specialist engineers, each with expertise in a specific field. Ultimately, the naval architect has to ensure that the final design is safe, on budget and seaworthy. To do this s/he uses high-level technology, computer-aided design and complex calculations to successfully bring together the final project.

The Person Specification

First and foremost, naval architects are keen to pursue a career in the maritime industry and are enthusiastic about boats/ships and the sea. In addition, they have to be interested in an engineering career, and although it may be possible to start as a shipyard apprentice and train up to the job, most entrants to this career have degrees or HND/Foundation degree qualifications in naval architecture, engineering, marine engineering, structural or civil engineering. You would need to be:

- technically minded with an interest in design, including detailed drawings and costings
- keen to work with computers to create simulations and 3D models
- interested in managing a project from the design stage to completion
- good at maths and physics
- able to visualise a design in a 3D way and be creative
- good at teamwork and managing a team in order to bring together a final project on time.

What It Takes

To be a chartered naval architect, you would need to have studied for an Honours degree recommended by the Royal Institution of Naval Architects (RINA). Experience in a design office or a shipyard is considered very useful. Those who train within the job as technician apprentices will at some stage have to gain degree-standard qualifications. A levels/Diploma level in maths/physics or similar subjects and a good GCSE profile with C grades and over or equivalent will be needed for entry to degree courses.

The International Institute of Marine Surveying (IIMS) accredits courses in maritime studies at the University of Portsmouth, including their Diploma in Marine Surveying.

What Else
Job opportunities vary according to the state of the shipbuilding market but vacancies tend to occur with design consultancies, shipbuilders, offshore drilling contractors, repair yards and the Ministry of Defence.

What It Pays
Salaries start at around £22,000 per year.

Prospects
The Maritime and Coastguard Agency (www.mcga.gov.uk) recruits experienced naval architects to be marine surveyors to assess the safety of ships and other marine structures. Self-employment, freelance or consultancy work is possible and some work is dependent on government contracts for military vessels like submarines.

Best Advice
Try some work experience at a shipbuilder's or shipyard. Work hard at maths, science and technology subjects. Take courses in computer-aided design at college. Check with RINA for recommended courses.

Contacts
The Royal Institution of Naval Architects, 10 Upper Belgrave Street, London SW1X 8BQ
020 7235 4622   www.rina.org.uk

The International Institute of Marine Surveying
www.iims.org.uk

Nutritionist (Dietitian)

Nutritionists are involved in research into and the promotion of the effects of diet on the growth, development and health of people and animals. They are often confused with dietitians, but although the training is similar for both jobs, nutritionists work privately, while dietitians are registered to work for the National Health Service. Nutritionists often work advising government or industry and use their knowledge of research to advise on food products and animal nutrition. With current public awareness of healthy eating initiatives, nutritionists are regularly consulted for informed opinions on anything to do with diet or nutrition.

The Job Description

As a nutritionist, you could be devising diets for improved physical performance for a football club or working for a large food manufacturer. You could be writing promotional leaflets on good nutrition, giving talks on healthy eating or be a media expert on eating or nutrition issues. Nutritionists are valuable to food manufacturers and large caterers in assessing the nutritional quality of the food supply. Some work on a freelance basis in an advisory or research capacity for major organisations. Others are involved in community health programmes and health promotion, which may be in the UK or abroad, particularly in Third World countries, for international relief agencies or for the United Nations.

For those nutritionists who have a recognised dietetics qualification, allowing them to be a state-registered dietitian, work in the National Health Service offers job opportunities in patient contact, ensuring the correct diet for hospital patients, or in advisory work to patients on changes of diet required by chronic conditions.

The Person Specification

Nutritionists need to have an interest in diet and food, good nutrition and people, but, because of the technical nature of the job, an aptitude for science, in particular chemistry, is essential. You would need:

- good communication skills, both written and verbal
- to be strong in sciences such as biology and chemistry
- a non-judgemental approach to patients, who may find it hard to take on board your dietary recommendations
- an ability to be persuasive, when necessary
- an understanding of scientific research and how it applies in real life.

What It Takes

There are specialist degree courses in dietetics that include state registration for National Health Service work. These take four years. With this type of qualification, you could work either as a nutritionist outside the health service or as a dietitian in hospitals; other nutrition degrees that do not offer state registration would be sufficient for non-health service work but may restrict some of your job opportunities, so research courses carefully, checking both nutrition, public health nutrition and dietetics courses on www.ucas.com.

There are also two-year postgraduate courses for science degree holders which offer state registration as a dietitian. All courses cover aspects of human nutrition, dietetics, food science and catering studies, sociology, psychology, biochemistry and physiology.

You will need five GCSEs or equivalent with A–C passes and 2–3 A levels/ Diploma or equivalent including chemistry and one other science to gain a place on nutrition or dietetics courses. There are also some combination courses offering nutrition and food science, biochemistry or physiology, but the British Dietetic Association can inform you of those that offer NHS state registration.

What Else

This is an expanding profession and job opportunities are generally good.

What It Pays

Salaries start at around £20,000 per year for nutritionists outside the NHS and within the NHS starting salaries for dieticians are £19,683 per year.

Prospects

There are good job opportunities and progression into teaching, research (particularly metabolic research for the control of illness by diet), work for food companies in product development, and in health education. Self-employment is also quite common.

Best Advice

Try and get some work experience in a food company with a food scientist or in a hospital with a dietitian.

Contacts

The Nutrition Society, 28 Portland Place, London W1B 1DE
020 7291 8378   www.nutritionsociety.org

The British Dietetic Association
www.bda.uk.com

NHS Careers
www.nhscareers.nhs.uk

Operating Department Practitioner (ODP)

Operating department practitioners (ODPs) work in the operating department alongside surgeons, anaesthetists and theatre nurses, with responsibilty for the anaesthetic, surgical and recovery phases of the operation. They might be preparing the patient for surgery, sterilising instruments for the operation or monitoring the patient after the operation.

The Job Description
In each phase of the operative procedure, the ODP will have different duties. In the pre-op phase this will include assisting the anaesthetist with equipment and devices that prepare the patient before the operation. During the operation, the ODP will wear a sterile gown and gloves and will work alongside the surgeon, preparing dressings, swabs and instruments for surgical procedures. Post-operatively, the ODP will monitor the recovery of the patient using specialist equipment.

The Person Specification
The ODP is an essential member of the health-care team for surgical and operative procedures, working within the NHS and the private medical sector. ODPs have a responsibility to provide high standards of patient care, as well as skilled support to the other members of the medical team. For this work you would need to be:

- interested in health care/health sciences
- practical and good with your hands
- able to work in life and death situations
- able to follow strict procedures within a surgical team
- prepared to undertake specialist training.

What It Takes
To start training as an ODP you will need five GCSE passes, C grade and above or equivalent, including maths, English language and a science. You will probably need two A levels/Diploma as well. You would be trained through a university course which has links with an NHS hospital or trust so that you learn the theory of operative care through the Diploma of Higher Education in Operating Department Practice, and would undertake practical placements at the same time in a clinical/ hospital setting. Most university courses take three years; in the first two years there will be an equal mix of theory relating to operative care and procedures, as well as practical experience as a trainee in an operating

department. In the third year, students are normally based in a hospital for most of the week and attend university on a day-release basis.

What Else

ODPs are recognised as being vital to the clinical team for operating departments and can also work as surgical assistants, in accident and emergency, in sterile supplies or on trauma teams.

Currently the NHS pays fees for ODP university courses and you will also receive an NHS bursary while training.

What It Pays

After qualifying, ODPs start on £17,000–£20,000 per year.

Prospects

There are opportunities for ODPs to work in a variety of areas within hospital services, including transplant teams, intensive care, patient transfers, resuscitation teams and in day surgery units.

Best Advice

Check the NHS website for detailed information about the work of ODPs. Be sure that you can cope with unpleasant sights, fluids and blood, as well as the need to perform swiftly and efficiently under pressure.

Contacts

College of Operating Department Practitioners, 197–199 City Road, London EC1V 1JN
0870 746 0984   www.aodp.org

NHS Careers
www.nhscareers.nhs.uk

Outdoor Pursuits Instructor

Outdoor pursuits instructors train people in a number of active outdoor sports such as climbing, canoeing, caving, kayaking and abseiling. As there is an element of danger to these sports, instructors have to be extremely well trained and qualified for this work. Outdoor centres who employ instructors have to be registered with the Adventurous Activities Licensing Authority (www.aals.org.uk) and must be able to guarantee that health and safety precautions are of paramount importance.

The Job Description

Instructors have to plan and deliver programmes of outdoor activities for a range of people including schoolchildren, youth clubs, family groups and even business people on team-building courses. They are normally skilled and qualified at more than one outdoor activity. They will also have to lead a group on excursions or expeditions and train group members in a variety of survival skills.

Most of the work involves careful planning of activities, taking into account group age, ability and confidence levels. Instructors have to motivate people and assess risk, always monitoring a range of factors such as an individual's ability levels, weather conditions and group dynamics.

The Person Specification

It is fairly obvious that this work would suit you if you love being outside and enjoy the thrill and calculated risk of outdoor pursuits. Remember that unpleasant weather conditions are pretty much guaranteed. As an instructor you would also have to be responsible for safety checks on equipment and have proper training in lifesaving, survival and first-aid.

You may start by enjoying a particular outdoor activity, such as abseiling or canoeing, as a hobby or interest, and may have trained through basic National Governing Board (NGB) competency courses. Each outdoor activity is governed by an NGB which monitors centres that offer outdoor courses. Once you are proficient at an outdoor sport (normally with at least one year's experience) you can progress to take different levels of instructor qualifications.

Instructors often have to work in the evenings, organising social activities for groups, and are therefore usually based in an outdoor education centre, where they may also live.

Instructors have to be extremely fit themselves, trained to instructor level in their individual sports and have first-aid certification. You will need to be:

- active with a lot of energy
- courageous when necessary
- calm in an emergency
- well organised
- patient when explaining skills to novices.

What It Takes

Instructors have to be highly proficient and experienced in their individual outdoor activities in the first place. Then they have to take instructor level qualifications recognised by the National Governing Board for each sport or activity that they instruct; for example, their skills might be accredited by the British Canoe Union or the Royal Yachting Association.

It is preferable to be trained to instruct in more than one activity, such as abseiling and mountaineering or canoeing and windsurfing, and there are a range of additional qualifications which will make you look even better when applying for jobs. For example at college level you may have the chance to take NVQ 2 in sport (Outdoor Activity and Leadership), or sports leadership or Duke of Edinburgh Awards. UK Sport offers the UK Coaching Certificate, a nationally recognised coaching qualification that may also be offered by particular NGBs – check www.sportscoachuk.org for details.

Outward Bound awards in outdoor education and leadership or the Community Sports Leader Award would also be extremely useful. Most outdoor centres value maturity and experience so any kind of volunteering or community activities will be helpful in making you stand out as a candidate for instructor vacancies.

University courses offering outdoor education specialisms may also be useful but make sure that they have both theory and practical sessions; the best ones allow you to take NGB awards in various outdoor pursuits and coaching qualifications at the same time. Look for courses with titles such as adventure sports coaching or outdoor leadership/education on www.ucas.com.

The Institute of Outdoor Learning also lists courses from basic instructor to advanced level, as well as those university courses that offer strong training and experience.

What Else

The Outward Bound organisation has trainee instructor opportunities for those with considerable experience in outdoor education and skill levels accredited by the various national governing bodies.

Duke of Edinburgh Awards at Gold and Silver level are also a good indication of commitment to this kind of work.

What It Pays

Jobs can be low paid and seasonal. Pay can range from £10,000 to £18,000 per year typically, although many jobs include free accommodation and food as part of the package. Work abroad is possible, especially for courses such as windsurfing or ski instructing (see Snowboard Instructor, page 195).

Prospects

There is a growth in this area due to personal development demands, particularly in large companies, encouraging leadership and teamwork.

There is great competition for senior outdoor education jobs and university qualifications in outdoor education in some form may be required for promotion opportunities. It is better if instructors can instruct in a number of activities, rather than just one skill.

Best Advice

Take recognised qualifications in a number of activities, talk to instructors and then decide if this is something you wish to take further. Check if your local college offers a course for the Community Sports Leader Award. Voluntary youth work including outdoor pursuits would be good experience. A clean driving licence (preferably a mini-bus licence) and Criminal Record Bureau clearance may also be required for this work.

Contacts

The Institute for Outdoor Learning, The Barn, Plumpton Old Hall, Plumpton, Penrith, Cumbria CA11 9NP
01768 885800   www.outdoor-learning.org

Sports Coach UK
www.sportscoachuk.org

Outward Bound centres are in various parts of the UK and are listed on the website at:
www.outwardbound.org.uk

Overseas Aid Worker

When you hear about an international crisis and see aid workers respond, you may wonder how people get into this kind of work. Well, some emergency aid workers work for a big-name charity such as Oxfam, others for less well-known projects. Some projects and development work is ongoing and not crisis driven. In general, a country in crisis does not need a well-meaning do-gooder; they need specialist help, and that is the reality of aid work today. In fact, the title 'aid worker' is rarely used, with job titles like project worker, development worker and nutrition adviser being more common.

The skills required can come from a wide range of specialisms including agriculture, health, education, water engineering, finance and disaster management.

The Job Description

There is probably no typical job in this type of work. Roles include work in refugee camps, the rebuilding of houses, the distribution of food, water and clothes, teaching in temporary schools, medical aid projects and agricultural advisory work.

For specialist professional roles in health, education or technical fields, professional qualifications, for example a teaching, civil engineering or agricultural economics degree, or a health promotion qualification/nursing degree, plus experience, will be required. Examples of medical jobs and some technical jobs can be seen on the Médecins Sans Frontières site (www.msf.org/unitedkingdom).

For project worker or development worker posts, specific expertise is required according to the scope of the project. For example, a project worker on a community health project would have health qualifications and experience in community health training. Often field experience and an in-depth knowledge of a particular developing country is demanded in job adverts. Horticultural or irrigation projects would require a development worker with horticultural/irrigation/water engineering qualifications and experience. Water/sanitation or flood projects would recruit water or flood engineers, and where communities need advice on sustainable agriculture, agricultural economists might be in demand.

Typically, jobs advertised require expertise and qualifications that are not readily available in developing, war-torn or disaster-hit countries. Most jobs require an ability to manage a situation under pressure, to motivate and support project staff and local people, to supervise resources and to be sensitive to the culture of the country.

The Person Specification

Apart from skills and expertise particular to the work undertaken, you would need to be:

- a good communicator
- able to work well in a team and on your own initiative
- self-motivated
- a good problem solver
- interested in working in cross-cultural situations
- interested in international development and the developing world.

What It Takes

You need to have a skill that is in demand in developing countries, so consider areas of health, education and technology such as water engineering and agricultural/horticultural advice. There are some specific degrees that may also be useful with titles like peace studies or international development studies. Check out courses that allow you to combine an unusual language such as Arabic or Swahili with your main degree study and find out if university exchange schemes offer the chance of study abroad in a developing country – check courses on www.ucas.com. Make sure that you gain some serious expertise in the area of your choice through high-level university study and through work experience, preferably abroad. Get involved with charities or Third World agencies in the UK as a volunteer in order to gain an in-depth knowledge of how they operate. Consider vacation or gap-year work from university that would give you the chance to experience a developing world country.

What Else

This work is not for the fainthearted or over-sensitive. It can involve long hours and be very demanding. Do some serious research through UK charities to see what they do. Be aware that competition for jobs is intense so you will need to prove more than just an idealistic commitment to this work – you must show that you can offer something unique and valuable in terms of skills, experience and knowledge.

Graduate internships, which may be unpaid, are possible with Oxfam (www.oxfam.org.uk) and Christian Aid (www.christianaid.org.uk) but you will need to stand out among the large numbers who apply for these.

What It Pays

As charities and agencies rely on donations and some government aid, salaries are never going to be huge, and typically start at £18,000–£25,000 per year.

Prospects

The Department for International Development (DFID) is the main UK government department concerned with international aid and it offers a graduate entry scheme. The United Nations (www.undp.org) and UNICEF (www.unicef.org) offer junior development programmes which are highly regarded routes into this work.

Relief operations manager and country representative posts for major charities and agencies offer good promotion possibilities for people with experience on the ground.

Best Advice

Consider Voluntary Service Overseas (VSO) or similar organisations as a way of working as a volunteer to check if this is the kind of work that interests you. The VSO Youth for Development programme would allow you to work abroad in a range of projects for one year – you would need one year's voluntary or community experience to apply for this programme.

These kinds of schemes or gap-year projects would provide you with a better understanding of the situation overseas, and allow you to gain valuable experience.

Contacts

The Department for International Development (DFID), 1 Palace Street, London SW1E 5HE
0845 300 4100   www.dfid.gov.uk

Voluntary Service Overseas, 317 Putney Bridge Road, London SW15 2PN
020 8780 7200   www.vso.org.uk

Médecins Sans Frontières (MSF)
www.msf.org/unitedkingdom

The Red Cross
www.redcross.org.uk

Charity Jobs
www.charityjob.co.uk

Packaging Designer

Packaging designers or technologists create great packaging ideas for a range of products. They are often part of the product design team that designed the product in the first place. It is recognised that the final packaging might have a huge impact on the ultimate marketability and sales of a product, so packaging designers have an important role to play. They have to take into account the nature of the product, the packaging needs, materials, artwork and costs of the packaging chosen.

The Job Description

Packaging designers work with product design teams from the beginning to determine the needs of the packaging component. Some goods need packaging for protection, others need it for purely marketing purposes, to stand out, for example, from competitor products. Some food products need robust packaging to maintain quality or freshness, and yet over-packaging is also a chief consideration. Designers will produce sample materials and test them out to work out what is most suitable; they may be simply practical solutions for packaging or they may be innovative designs that make that product unique and desirable. A variety of computer-aided design packages will be used to produce prototypes which can then be market tested.

The Person Specification

This work suits people who are keen on design and interested in solving the problems presented by the demands of packaging. You would need to like graphics and visual design and be interested in the technology of how things are created or engineered. To do this work, you would need to be:

- creative and design focused
- practical, with the ability to work well in a project team
- focused on detail and how small adjustments can make a difference
- aware of the business need for packaging and the cost implications.

What It Takes

Most people would train through a specialist degree course in graphics and packaging or product design. Courses such as the one at Ravensbourne College (www.ravensbourne.ac.uk) offer training in computer-based design, usability studies and work on live projects (from leading manufacturing employers). For degree courses, a good GSCE profile or equivalent, with C grades and over in English, maths and science, plus A level/Diploma in subjects such as graphic design or art, would be needed.

The Institute of Packaging also offers certificate and diploma courses for the technology side of packaging.

What Else

Designers spend some time based in an office using design packages, while other time might be spent doing laboratory or production line testing, involving planning and running stress/wear tests on packaging prototypes to check for suitability of design.

What It Pays

Starting salaries range from £15,000–£20,000 per year.

Prospects

Paper engineering for pop-up books and maps might be a possible career progression from this, if your design skills are advanced.

Best Advice

Work hard at graphics and technology subjects. Start noticing the variety of types of packaging and consider the need for environmentally friendly packaging solutions.

Contacts

Institute of Packaging: the Packaging Society, Institute of Materials, Minerals and Mining, Springfield House, Springfield Business Park, Grantham, Lincolnshire NG31 7BG
www.pi2.org.uk

Paramedic

Paramedics are the highest qualified members of an emergency and accident ambulance crew and normally have at least two years' experience at ambulance technician grade. Ambulance crews for emergency and accident work are made up of ambulance care assistants, ambulance technicians (sometimes called emergency medical technicians) and paramedics. Ambulance care assistants drive the ambulance and are qualified in lifting, handling and basic first aid. They generally work for the patient transport service, conveying non-urgent patients to hospitals or day centres. Ambulance technicians are qualified to drive the ambulance and offer pre-hospital emergency care.

Paramedics are trained to use a number of advanced skills in emergency situations, such as drug therapy, reading ECGs (charts that record the electrical activity of the heart), defibrillation machines (using electrical shock to stimulate the heart), inserting drips and airway management (putting a tube into the windpipe).

The Job Description
Paramedics are responsible for diagnosing, treating and stabilising patients at the scene of an accident or as a result of a sudden illness. They are trained in emergency treatment techniques using a range of monitoring equipment. While the work can range from road accidents to minor injuries, one crucial personality characteristic needed for this work is the quick thinking required in these stressful situations.

The Person Specification
The work is varied and demanding and requires advanced techniques in life support using a range of emergency care equipment. Paramedics have to be able to stay calm under pressure, make good decisions and deal with patients and their families. Frequently, they can be exposed to dangerous situations, from road accidents to domestic violence disputes and drunken, aggressive patients. They often work in partnership with other emergency services such as the fire service and the police. You will need to be:

- physically fit and active
- in possession of a clean driving licence
- able to pass a selection test including a lifting and carrying assessment
- genuinely interested in caring for people
- a good communicator
- interested in health and, ideally, knowledgeable about anatomy.

What It Takes

Some paramedics train as ambulance technicians and after 1–2 years' experience can apply for trainee paramedic posts. For ambulance technician work most ambulance services require four GCSEs grades A–C or equivalent. In-service training normally involves intensive courses on the respiratory, cardiovascular and nervous systems, and physiology and anatomy, which may be through a university Foundation degree or similar. Further training and exams follow in diagnosis and assessment techniques and both the theory and practice of pre-hospital medicine. After final exams and completion of training, paramedics are granted registration by the NHS.

If you're interested in this work you could also take the full-time university route into paramedic work which involves a degree (three years) or Foundation degree (two years) in Paramedical Sciences and includes spending about 40 per cent of the time on placement with an ambulance service. For Honours degree entry you would need GCSEs in English, maths and a science C grade or above (or equivalent) and two A levels/ Diploma or equivalent. Foundation degree entry is possible for applicants with the same GCSE or equivalent profile and one A level or equivalent.

What Else

Every ambulance for emergency work has to have at least one trained paramedic. Shift work, unsocial hours and weekend work are an essential part of the job. This is an extremely popular career – when ambulance services advertise they are often inundated with applications so you will need to get the best qualifications and experience you can to stand out from the field.

What It Pays

NHS pay rates start at £18,698–£24,198 per year for paramedics, with extra allowances for unsocial hours.

Prospects

Paramedics can be promoted to supervisory work, to management grades or to ambulance control room work.

Best Advice

Get caring experience of some kind, through voluntary or paid work. Learn First Aid with the St John Ambulance (www.sja.org.uk) or the Red Cross (www.redcross.org.uk). Find out if your local ambulance service has a First Responder voluntary service – First Responder volunteers are trained to respond to emergency situations in their neighbourhood area.

Pay attention to your own physical fitness. Study health-related subjects and anatomy. Some colleges offer pre-services or public services courses, which have units on paramedic training.

Contacts

The British Paramedic Association, 28 Wilfrid Street, Derby DE23 8GF
01332 746356   www.britishparamedic.org

NHS Careers
www.nhscareers.nhs.uk

Patent Examiner

The Job Description

Once someone has an idea or comes up with an invention, they need to protect it (their intellectual property) by seeking a patent or copyright, and this is processed through the UK Intellectual Property Office. A patent examiner at this office will be responsible for assessing applications for patents and awarding the patent, which means that the inventor has a legal monopoly for making and selling the invention for 20 years.

The Person Specification

Patent examiners work for the UK Intellectual Property Office in Wales, checking an inventor's specifications and conducting searches through applications to check if an invention is unique. They then write reports, which are sent to the applicant or the patent agent who is acting for the applicant. Due to the technical nature of many patent applications, patent examiners have to be analytical and able to understand scientific concepts. You would need to be:

- logical and analytical
- scientific and a problem solver
- decisive
- able to write precise technical descriptions
- able to read French and German (basic knowledge is required, with further training in the job)
- able to use succinct English in precise legal terms.

Patent agents/attorneys check that an invention is original and prepare a specification for submission to the UK Intellectual Property Office. They may represent their client in negotiations with the patent examiner and may appear in court as an expert witness in the case of legal disputes over trademarks, designs or copyright.

What It Takes

Patent examiners and agents have to have degrees in science, medical sciences, electrical engineering, maths or similar scientific/technological subjects to be accepted for training. Many patent agents have trained with the UK Intellectual Property Office as examiners and then progress to work as patent agents after experience. More advanced knowledge of French and German is considered very desirable and useful, as patents experts have to be able to check European patents as well. There are some degree courses that allow study for a science or technical degree with a language as a subsidiary subject, and these might be very suitable. Otherwise vacation time spent abroad in Europe could develop language skills, and there are other university programmes sponsored by the EU which allow students to benefit from European study and language skill development.

For science, maths or technology degree courses 2–3 A levels/Diploma or equivalent in maths or the sciences are normally required. IT skills are also part of these jobs, so would need to be developed to as high a level as possible.

Patent examiners undergo 1–2 years' on-the-job training with the UK Intellectual Property Office, supervised by a senior examiner.

Patent agents start in graduate posts, often with large manufacturing companies, and are trained for 3–4 years, after which they have to pass the qualifying exams for the Register of Patent Agents through the Chartered Institute of Patent Agents. Once qualified, they can call themselves a patent agent or a registered trade-mark agent.

What Else
Competition for graduate training with the UK Intellectual Property Office is intense, so degree classification (probably 2.i and above) and even good A level/Diploma level points scores will be crucial. Most employers offer language training as part of the initial training period.

What It Pays
Patent examiners start on £21,000–£24,000 per year. Patent agents are paid according to their success in applications for patents, but trainees start on about £20,000 per year.

Prospects
Patent examiners and agents are part of a relatively small profession so competition for jobs is fierce. The UK Intellectual Property Office normally holds a graduate recruitment process on a yearly basis. Opportunities also exist for work abroad through the European Patent Office or the World Intellectual Property Organization in Geneva, and patent experts can broaden their experience by moving into specialist work on trade-mark designs, copyright or intellectual property, with the chance of earning extremely high salaries for their specialist expertise.

Best Advice
Maximise your potential by working hard at scientific and technical subjects, and don't forget your languages – most employers will expect you to be able to read and speak English, French and German. Take a look at the summer internship programme for undergraduates offered by the World Intellectual Property Organization – this would be ideal experience.

Contacts

UK Intellectual Property Office, Concept House, Cardiff Road, Newport, South Wales NP10 8QQ
0845 950 0505   www.ipo.gov.uk

European Patent Office
www.epo.org

World Intellectual Property Organization, Geneva
www.wipo.org

Chartered Institute of Patents Agents
www.cipa.org.uk

Perfusionist

This job has nothing to do with perfume, and although it may seem unfamiliar, it is likely that you have seen a perfusionist at work if you are the kind of person who likes to watch live medical operations demonstrating techniques such as open-heart surgery on television.

It is, in fact, a highly skilled, technical and scientific job; a perfusionist might be called a medical technical officer (MTO) or a clinical scientist within hospital services. Perfusionists are members of the open-heart surgery team, with chief responsibility for the heart–lung machinery. They may also be involved with a range of major operations such as heart–lung surgeries and organ transplants. They are not doctors, but are vital to the work of cardiac surgeons, as they operate the artificial heart pumps that replace the heart's function while the surgeon operates. The perfusionist has to know how to use mechanical and electronic equipment to ensure oxygen reaches the patient's body through the blood, even when the lungs and heart are not working due to the operation's procedures.

The Job Description

The perfusionist is a skilled health professional who is trained as a member of the surgical team to set up and operate the heart–lung machinery, including autotransfusion units that prevent blood loss during operations. When a patient's heart has to be stopped in open-heart surgery, the patient's blood has to be taken out of the body, oxygenated and returned to the body through the heart–lung machine. The perfusionist is responsible for the operation of this machine during surgery and has to monitor circulation, take action if required and communicate with the surgeon and anaesthetist. Equipment used is highly technological and may be mechanical or electronic. Perfusionists literally do hold a patient's life in their hands.

There are many artificial replacements for a patient's failing organs and a perfusionist is an essential part of the medical team that undertakes these major surgeries; they are involved in artificial lung, heart, kidney and liver operations and help in the treatment of coronary artery disease, heart valve disease and kidney failure, as well as heart and lung transplants.

The Person Specification

A perfusionist has to use knowledge of anatomy, physiology, chemistry, physics and electronics to operate life-support procedures during surgery. You would need to be:

- comfortable in life or death situations, especially in operating theatres
- able to work efficiently as part of a medical team

- manually dextrous
- able to work with highly technical machinery
- interested in health
- able to maintain concentration and energy levels for the lengthy operations (often 12–15 hours)
- able to work under pressure and be quick thinking.

What It Takes
Most perfusionists have degree level qualifications in a science such as biology, chemistry or biomedical sciences, and then obtain a trainee post in the NHS and train through a work-based route which involves further study for postgraduate qualifications in clinical science (perfusion). A levels/Diploma in sciences and a good GCSE profile with C grades and above will be required for entry onto degree courses. Take a look at the Postgraduate Diploma in Clinical Sciences (Perfusion), which is run on a block-release basis at the North East Surrey College (NESCOT) (www.nescot.ac.uk) to give you an idea of this area of study.

What Else
Most jobs are in the health service, but you will have to be alert to advertised vacancies, which may be on the NHS Careers website, in local newspapers or in hospital vacancy bulletins. Jobs may be advertised as trainee perfusionist or MTO. This is a small profession (with only a few vacancies advertised each year) and jobs will mainly be available in major hospitals that have units or expertise for major operations and procedures.

What It Pays
NHS pay rates start at between £19,166 and £24,803 per year.

Prospects
Career progression through further/specialist training and study is possible for an MSc in perfusion science. Work abroad is also possible.

Best Advice
Research this career carefully and try and talk to someone who does the job. Work hard at all sciences and cultivate a strong interest in anatomy and health.

Contacts
Society of Clinical Perfusionists of Great Britain and Ireland, Royal College of Surgeons, 35–43 Lincoln's Inn Fields, London WC2A 3PE
020 7869 6891   www.sopgbi.org

NHS Careers
www.nhscareers.nhs.uk

Personal Trainer

Personal trainers work in gyms, fitness centres, health farms/clubs and leisure centres, helping their clients to become fitter and healthier through assessment programmes which they plan and deliver. These programmes might involve using specific machines, weights, exercises and customised plans tailored to an individual's needs and fitness levels.

The Job Description

Instructors or trainers have to be knowledgeable about fitness and exercise and be able to recommend the right exercise and fitness plan to their client. They would do a diagnostic fitness assessment, discuss lifestyle, nutrition and weight management, and then make suitable suggestions, according to the individual's needs. They may work with individuals or with groups. Group sessions may take the form of specific fitness classes like aerobics, step, keep fit, yoga or other exercise and movement instruction. Some gyms specialise in classes for the over-50s or they may offer sports massage or injury clinics. Being an instructor/trainer requires patience and an ability to assess clients and then pace exercise programmes accordingly. A personal trainer may work in a gym or leisure centre or be freelance and visit people in their homes. Some companies offer a personal trainer service as a work benefit for staff.

The Person Specification

There are many specialisms for instructors in this work, but the personal qualities required are almost more important than skill at a particular activity. You would need to be:

- fit and healthy and committed to good health yourself
- really interested in helping people improve their levels of fitness
- able to motivate people
- knowledgeable about anatomy and physiology
- able to assess and recognise health problems.

What It Takes

There are many different specialist courses for this kind of work but to be recognised and accredited you would need to be on the Register of Exercise Professionals (REP) which recommends courses at Level 3 (A level/Diploma equivalent) as a minimum.

Level 3 courses are available through colleges and private fitness organisations – most will be called Personal Trainer Level 3 but they may actually be a package of useful qualifications covering cardiovascular assessment, resistance training, gym instruction, exercise and nutrition. They often take a year of part-time study. Most courses include units on anatomy and physiology, types of exercise and warm-ups and warm-downs, safe training techniques, and coaching and leading groups.

The YMCA qualifications are well regarded and available at colleges or through intensive courses at locations throughout the UK. In addition, NVQs in sport and recreation at Level 2 and/or 3 will probably be available at a local college, either full time or on a day-release basis for apprentices in leisure centres or gyms. Specialist training in fitness would then be needed to top up the NVQs to a Level 3 fitness qualification. It is possible to gain entry to NVQ Level 2 with GCSEs at D grade or equivalent, but most Level 3 courses require GCSEs in English, maths and a science at C grade or equivalent.

University Foundation or Honours degree courses in sports or exercise science (see www.ucas.com) are also a possible route into this work and REP offers entry to their register for university degree holders. Some universities offer specialist additional qualifications in fitness as part of their degree programmes.

What Else
Most gyms and fitness centres are open day and night with classes and personal trainer sessions available to suit customer demands, so unsocial hours and shift work are an essential part of this job.

What It Pays
Typically, salaries in gyms and fitness centres start at around £18,000–£24,000 per year. Freelance trainers may earn a hourly rate of £20–£40 per hour, or more if they manage to gain a reputation with wealthy or famous clients.

Prospects
Many people are booking sessions with a personal trainer in their own homes, so work opportunities are expanding. There is an ever-increasing interest in exercise and general fitness as a means of promoting well-being, and this has led to an upsurge of jobs for fitness professionals.

Best Advice
Join a gym and work on your own fitness. Talk to instructors and trainers.

Contacts
The Register of Exercise Professionals (REP), 8–10 Crown Hill, Croydon, Surrey CR10 1RS
020 8686 6464   www.exerciseregister.com

YMCAfit
www.ymcafit.org.uk

Phlebotomist

Phlebotomists are generally specialist medical laboratory assistants working in the NHS who collect blood from patients for diagnostic examination in laboratories. They may take blood samples on hospital wards, in surgeries or in clinics and take samples back to a pathology lab for testing and analysis.

The Job Description

Blood samples taken by phlebotomists can help in haematological diagnoses, in tests on the immune system, or in blood transfusion work. Taking blood from a vein (venous blood samples) can be complicated by the patient's anxiety, sunken veins and medical conditions connected with blood pressure. Phlebotomists have to choose the best site for taking the blood (venepuncture), using a needle to draw off just the right amount. They then have to apply a dressing and label the sample carefully to avoid any mix-ups of samples. They could be dealing with a baby or an elderly person and must be reassuring and calm.

Some people with a phobia of needles can be terrified at the idea of having to have a blood test. Phlebotomists need to be skilled at dealing with all eventualities in order to help patients overcome their fear.

The Person Specification

Phlebotomists work as part of a health-care team under the supervision of the pathology lab and medical professionals, but they are the experts in taking the exact blood samples needed to aid diagnosis. For this work you would need to be:

- interested in health and the diagnosis and prevention of disease
- good with your hands and able to undertake a technical process
- focused on accuracy and detail to label and transport blood samples according to strict procedures
- sensitive to individual patients
- calm and gentle in dealing with patients.

What It Takes

The NHS trains phlebotomists through a six-month medical laboratory assistant training course within hospitals, offering NVQs at Level 2 and 3 in health (Blood Donor Support). A minimum of two GCSEs with C grades and over or equivalent are generally required, probably including maths, English and science.

Flexibility is important as cover is sometimes required at weekends and bank holidays.

What Else

Phlebotomists have to ensure that specimens of blood are taken correctly and not harmed during collection, otherwise test results will be worthless. Their place of work may vary according to where the patients are located, so they may visit wards, clinics, medical centres or accident and emergency departments.

What It Pays

NHS pay rates start at £12,500–£15,500 per year.

Prospects

With training, phlebotomists can move into other areas of pathology, such as cervical screening programmes and treatment/monitoring of heart problems and function. They can also work for the National Blood Service, the voluntary blood donation service for the UK.

Best Advice

Be sure that you can deal with the sight of blood and be responsible for a medical process that is important in the diagnosis of disease.

Contacts

Institute of Biomedical Science, 12 Coldbath Square, London EC1R 5HL
020 7713 0214   www.ibms.org

National Association of Phlebotomists
www.phlebotomy.org

NHS Careers
www.nhscareers.nhs.uk

Picture Researcher

If you've ever wondered just how the pictures, photos or images that appear in your favourite newspaper or magazine are sourced, then here is the answer. As a general rule, pictures are stored in picture libraries or are commissioned specifically from photographers; it is the job of the picture researcher to source the right picture for an article or feature from one or other of these sources. Picture researchers can work, therefore, alongside journalists on magazines, for publishers, for a photo agency, or freelance for a range of media and related companies.

The Job Description
Picture researchers can be employed by museums, specialist picture/photo libraries, newspapers, magazines or publishing companies to find, produce and buy the rights to particular photos or images. To do this they have to have a wide-ranging knowledge of artistic and photo images, whether it be a particular photo of a celebrity or a famous painting.

They have to deal with individual photographers, specialist libraries, photo agencies and a network of other companies and people who they know can give them access to the best images. As many images are now available online, they have to know how to use digital technology, be aware of copyright infringement and be able to advise their clients on how best to source images legally.

A picture researcher will have their own contacts list, often called their 'contact book', so that they can phone round and source a picture at great speed. If they are working for a picture library or agency, they might be assessing photos that come in from photographers and negotiating picture rights (the legal right to reproduce a picture in a magazine or journal), or searching through their sources (often on the internet or by using specific databases) for a picture required by a customer/client or for a museum or exhibition.

The Person Specification
Images and photos are constantly bombarding us from adverts and hoardings, but picture researchers have to be able to remember the exact details of a picture/photo, its possible impact and potential use, and its copyright or source. They have to be able to recognise a particular photographer's style and make decisions about finding an image to suit their brief (what their client or employer is asking for) or commission a photographer to produce a particular image. For this work you would need to have:

- an almost perfect photographic memory
- a strong interest in visual media, that is, photos, paintings, adverts, digital images

- negotiating and business skills to liaise with photographers, picture libraries and news/photo agencies
- organisational skills to keep track of contacts and to be able to source different pictures from a range of contacts
- digital media/information technology skills to use specialist software with confidence
- networking/communication skills to make and keep good contacts for future searches.

What It Takes

Most picture researchers have a background in fine art, photography or visual media, and job adverts normally demand graduates from art/history or 'art-type courses', so it would be recommended that you take GCSEs/A levels/Diploma, preferably in subjects like art, textiles, history, and then study a degree course in art, history or visual media, or a combination of these subjects.

That probably won't be enough, though, as this is a competitive market for jobs, and picture libraries, agencies, magazines or museums who employ picture researchers normally want other skills and experience according to their specialism. So, museums will ask for museum experience and even a foreign language, while magazines may ask for journalism experience. This may seem a little demanding, but you will have to make sure that you gain suitable relevant experience depending on the kind of picture research you want to do. This might mean working for free at a museum or on a magazine in vacations. For example a museum such as the Victoria and Albert Museum (www.vam.ac.uk) in London advertised recently for an unpaid volunteer administrator/researcher to work in its picture library for a four-month period.

What Else

There are short specialist courses and postgraduate courses for graduates or those interested in this work, which could help by giving you the relevant skills to be a convincing job applicant. It might be worth checking courses offered by the London School of Publishing and the Publishing Training Centre at Book House. The Publishing Training Centre offers a distance-learning picture researcher course and the London School of Publishing offers an intensive two-day course in picture research. Even a one-day course in picture research at the London College of Communication at the University of the Arts may be useful to build your confidence.

In addition, most employers look for specific skills in computer design packages, such as Adobe Photoshop, Adobe Illustrator and QuarkXPress, so make sure to pick up these skills through short courses at a local college.

What It Pays

This can vary tremendously according to where you are working and whether you are working freelance for a museum or for a magazine. However, starting salaries might be around £15,000–£18,000 per year.

Prospects

There are so many different specialisms within this work, from finding travel photos to environmental or nature photography, to fashion, to lifestyle or architecture, that career prospects can be wide ranging.

Best Advice

Start taking note now of visual images you see around you and compile a portfolio of photos and images. Make a note of the sources and which photographer or picture agency is credited. Learn to download pictures from the internet and check out the photo sources that are on the web. Take a digital photography course and visit museums and picture libraries. Research university courses (www.ucas.com) that will help you learn the skills you need, and develop the photographic visual memory that is essential in this work.

Contacts

British Association of Picture Libraries and Agencies, 18 Vine Hill, London EC1R 5DZ
020 7713 1211   www.bapla.org.uk

Picture Research Association
www.picture-research.org.uk

London School of Publishing
www.publishing-school.co.uk

The Publishing Training Centre at Book House
www.train4publishing.co.uk

London College of Communication, University of the Arts
www.lcc.arts.ac.uk

Playworker/Play Therapist

Many people consider careers in childcare, including jobs in nurseries or schools, but there is a growing trend to employ playworkers at after-school and pre-school play clubs, and in therapy work with children in hospital and social services. The value of structured or ad hoc play is extremely valuable for all children and the availability of trained playwork professionals is seen as vitally important. Playwork can increasingly be a part of existing childcare jobs or a job in itself.

The Job Description

Playworkers work with babies and children up to the age of about 11, organising a variety of creative, sport-related and fun activities which stimulate, challenge and relax children. The emphasis is on play as a means of drawing children out, helping them to socialise and to stretch them as individuals. Playworkers may work in children's centres, inner-city play centres, in country areas through the provision of a travelling playbus, in pre-and after-school play clubs or in hospitals and health centres.

Pre- and after-school play clubs are a boon to parents who find it difficult to work within school start and finish times. Breakfast clubs may even be offered. The play clubs may be attached to primary schools or in community centres.

Hospital playworkers will specialise in play for sick children, finding the best way to incorporate play as an activity bearing in mind restrictions caused by the illness or the health condition of the child.

Play therapists work with children who have particular mental health problems or who have suffered trauma or abuse. They find a way for these children to communicate and express themselves through the medium of play and plan programmes of play which will support recovery.

The Person Specification

Playworkers have a strong belief in the value of play and an interest in children and child development. You would have to be:

- able to build rapport with children easily
- sensitive to children's needs
- a good communicator with children and their parents
- prepared to pass a Criminal Records Bureau police check
- creative in coming up with ideas for play activities that children will enjoy and learn from.

In certain hospital or therapy situations, playworkers or play therapists may have to work within a team of health service or social service professionals to help support the particular needs of an individual child. Play therapy may help children come to terms with stressful or frightening events and therefore an interest in psychology and counselling is needed for this more complex play therapy role.

What It Takes

For **general playwork** in nurseries or children's centres, you will need a recognised childcare qualification such as the CACHE diplomas and certificates or the BTEC National Diplomas or NVQs in childcare, preferably at Levels 2 and 3; however, there are separate NVQs in playwork at Levels 1, 2 and 3, which would also be useful. These are available at most colleges and entry requirements are normally 3–4 GCSEs at C grade and over, or equivalent, including English and maths. NVQs can also be taken while working in a childcare setting and through an apprenticeship in childcare.

For **hospital playwork**, specialist courses are available at some colleges which will train you to be Hospital Play Staff Education Trust (HPSET) qualified – these cover the theory and practice of play and hospital play projects. For entry to an HPSET course, you will need a recognised childcare qualification such as a BTEC National Diploma and at least three years' experience with children. The HPSET website lists colleges which have recognised courses.

For **play therapy**, you would need a relevant degree in psychology, social work, teaching, occupational therapy or something similar and then follow this with a postgraduate diploma in play therapy. This type of course is offered by universities including Roehampton University, the University of York, Liverpool Hope University College and the University of Reading – see the British Association of Play Therapists for further details.

What Else

Child protection work and the recognition of signs of abuse are a key part of childcare, along with appropriate support of children with special educational needs.

What It Pays

Starting salaries for playworkers are around £12,000–£20,000 per year. Play therapists earn in the region of £19,000–£24,000 per year.

Prospects

There are possibilities of career progression into hospital play therapy, childcare manager posts for a local council, social work, child protection work or teaching.

Best Advice

Most people start by volunteering at a school or playgroup or by taking a 'Parents as Educators' course, available through some primary schools.

Contacts

Children's Workforce Development Council (CWDC), 2nd Floor, 11 Albion Street, Leeds LS1 5EJ
0113 244 6311   www.cwdcouncil.org.uk

British Association of Play Therapists, 31 Cedar Drive, Keynsham, Bristol BS31 2TY
01179 860390   www.bapt.uk.com

National Association of Hospital Play Staff
www.nahps.org.uk

Hospital Play Staff and Education Trust (HPSET)
www.hpset.co.uk

Prosthetist

This is one of the less well-known jobs in the medical field, and because it is concerned with replacement limbs or body parts it can seem a bit strange or even gory. Nonetheless, for all sorts of reasons, including landmines and road accidents, people suffer the loss of a limb or an eye, for example, and prosthetists perform a vital service in designing and fitting artificial limbs or parts to help a patient lead as active a life as possible.

The Job Description

Prosthetists are part of a rehabilitation team and are involved in assessing a patient to see what will be required to enable that person to manage without a particular limb or body part. An orbital prosthetist might take measurements and place a special mould or cast in the empty eye socket to ensure that a false eye will fit perfectly. Once the new eye is made, according to the specifications taken by the prosthetist, the orbital prosthetist will fit the eye and advise on its care. Similarly, in fitting a new limb, the prosthetist will talk to the patient and take detailed measurements and shape-sensing tracings so that the design of the false limb can be as perfect as possible. Further adjustments have to be made at the fitting stage, and repairs or changes can be made as the patient becomes used to the appliance or false limb/part.

The Person Specification

This may seem a strange job but, as you can imagine, it is highly important and satisfying to help and support patients through what might seem to be an embarrassing and discomforting process. You would need to be:

- extremely sensitive/tactful and aware of the feelings of those going through the pain of losing a limb or body part
- practical and good with your hands in handling technical equipment and measuring devices
- a good communicator in explaining to patients the procedures and processes that they will undergo
- interested in how the body works and biomechanics.

What It Takes

To be a fully qualified prosthetist, you will need to be state registered. This will mean taking a recognised degree course in prosthetics – the two main courses in the UK are at the University of Salford and the University of Strathclyde. To gain a place on these courses you will need GCSEs at C grade and above, or equivalent, in English, maths and physics/combined science, and two or three A levels/Diploma, or equivalent – maths and/or physics and/or biology are the preferred subjects.

What Else

It may be possible to do some work-shadowing at your local hospital with prosthetists, physiotherapists or occupational therapists, which could be valuable experience for this kind of career. The NHS is one potential employer of prosthetists, although many work for private prosthetics companies.

What It Pays

Starting salaries for newly trained prosthetists are around £23,500 per year.

Prospects

Work abroad in developing countries is a possibility, especially in caring for people harmed by landmines.

Best Advice

You might try to design a disability aid as part of a design technology project at school and this would give you a good idea of the issues to consider when working with patients in need of a prosthesis.

Contacts

The British Association of Prosthetists and Orthotists, Sir James Clark Building, Abbey Mill Business Centre, Paisley PA1 1TJ
0141 561 7217   www.bapo.com

Department of Rehabilitation, University of Salford
www.salford.ac.uk

National Centre for Training and Education in Prosthetics and Orthotics, University of Strathclyde
www.strath.ac.uk/prosthetics

Radio Producer

A radio producer is responsible for the whole process that gets a radio programme on air. This includes coming up with the initial idea for a feature, researching potential ideas or slots, thinking up new angles and technical know-how. The final output could be a small news item or a themed section. Depending on whether the focus is music or current affairs, or local radio with its varied mix, the producer will make decisions on the target audience's interests, edit and write news items, plan segments and insert adverts where necessary. For music stations, it is often the producer in conjunction with the DJ who decides the playlist (the music sequence that will be played).

The Job Description

Radio producers divide their time according to the nature of their employer and their contract, but typically they will come up with programme ideas or themed segments, plan the structure of a programme (timed to the last minute), brief presenters or DJs, deal with listener surveys and manage a team of technical and creative staff who produce the programme. Work has often to be planned in advance according to the time of year, celebrations and events, but producers also have to respond to sudden circumstances or emergencies when required. Some producers work for independent companies who bid for particular programmes, while others may work full time for a particular radio station.

The Person Specification

As producers need a range of skills, talent and experience, they need to be flexible and able to deal with a technical problem, a planning meeting or a people-crisis with equal expertise. For this work, you would need to be:

- able to write scripts and briefings for presenters
- able to research or commission research when required and make sense of it
- adept at timing radio slots, whether they be music slots and/or current affairs or phone-ins
- able to manage a team of technicians, creatives and researchers
- extremely well organised and able to plan well in advance
- able to respond well to pressure and deadlines
- fascinated by radio as a medium with its particular characteristics.

What It Takes

While some people start off as research assistant/broadcast assistant and then progress into radio production work, others may come through the technical route from the engineering side. Journalism is one way into this work and there is also a highly popular and competitive scheme run by the BBC for trainee producers. With thousands of applicants for many BBC jobs, many people decide to start in local or hospital radio, working for free and then applying for production assistant jobs with local or national radio stations. Another useful way to gain experience is through CSV Media (www.csv. org.uk/services/Media) who run the Action Desks for the BBC at their local radio stations. Volunteers with the Action Desks are trained to collect, edit and compile stories and information about community events which are then scripted and presented live by volunteers on BBC local radio.

A specialised broadcast journalism or radio journalism degree/Foundation degree course could be useful for this work, so check courses available through www.ucas.com – good courses normally offer training at a university radio station or through local radio as a placement. University courses normally expect A levels/Diploma in subjects such as media, English or even technical subjects plus a good GCSE profile with maths, English and science at C grade or above, or equivalent.

What is certain is that you will need to be determined and motivated and any course of training or placement experience you can get will help you in job applications. The BBC has a work placement scheme in various departments that is really worth considering – look on www.bbc.co.uk/workexperience.

What Else

Working hours can be long with high levels of stress. Short contracts and freelance work are common.

What It Pays

This varies, as much of the work is freelance, but typical salaries are in the range of £16,000–£30,000 per year. Local or community-based radio stations may pay less than this.

Prospects

Promotion to senior producer or to producer for a more prestigious programme is possible with experience.

Best Advice

Get involved in hospital radio or in a college or university radio station. Journalistic experience for a school, college or university newspaper is also valuable. Use contacts from work placements (e.g. at the BBC) to find out about upcoming jobs, or at least to help you get sight of the BBC internal vacancies paper, *Ariel*.

Check the Skillset and Broadcast Journalism Training Council sites for information about the industry and recommended training, the Radio Academy (www.radioacademy.org) and Grapevine (www.grapevinejobs. co.uk) for jobs, the Hospital Radio site to find local hospitals wanting volunteers (www.hospitalradio.co.uk), and if you fancy being involved in the production of traffic bulletins then consider being an Information Editor for Trafficlink (www.trafficlink.co.uk).

Contacts

Skillset, Prospect House, 21 Caledonian Road, London N1 9GB
020 7713 9800   www.skillset.org

BBC Recruitment
www.bbc.co.uk/jobs and www.bbc.co.uk/newtalent

Broadcast Journalism Training Council
www.bjtc.org.uk

National Union of Journalists
www.nuj.org.uk

Revenue and Customs Officer

When you think of customs and excise work, you may think of something thrilling and exciting, even dangerous, connected to smuggling; it is worth realising that although some customs officers do this kind of work, most do not. Many customs and revenue officers are involved in VAT work, that is, collecting the correct amount of money from businesses on behalf of the government or making sure businesses pay duty on goods that they import. Others' work might be at airports or ports, ensuring that illegal activities are prevented.

The Job Description

There are three main types of customs and excise officers:

VAT officers who visit local businesses to check that they are accounting for VAT properly according to the relevant laws. About 40 per cent of customs and excise officers are VAT officers.

Excise and inland customs officers who visit business premises like distilleries, oil refineries and importers to ensure that regulations are being followed correctly and that the correct amount of duty is being paid.

Customs officers who have a responsibility to prevent smuggling and to ensure that health and trade regulations are obeyed. They are the face of customs work in some ways, as we see them at airports, checking bags and clearing passengers through security. They wear uniforms and work shifts.

The Person Specification

Customs and revenue officers collect over 40 per cent of central government taxation every year through VAT, customs duties on goods entering the country and excise duties on goods like petrol, alcohol and tobacco. You would be employed by a major government department and would need to be:

- a good communicator, with an ability to relate well to many different types of people and personalities
- organised and able to manage your own workload
- able to question and challenge people and pay attention to documentation
- prepared to work indoors or outdoors
- able to explain and apply rules and regulations in a fair and firm manner
- equipped with analytical and investigative skills, particularly for VAT work.

What It Takes

You would need to enter Her Majesty's Revenue and Customs (HMRC), probably at officer grade. Some applicants will start at administrative assistant level and move up the grades to become a customs officer. Vacancies are advertised on the HMRC website. At administrative levels you would need at least five GCSE pass grades at C grade and over, or equivalent, including English and maths. For customs officer levels, normally A levels/Diploma or equivalent and/or degree level qualifications are needed. Typical degree subject study might be in public services or criminology.

What Else

Undercover or surveillance work, and occasional court appearances, might be part of the work of a customs official. However, in essence, most customs officers are responsible for ensuring the government gets its revenue or taxation and that revenue is protected from illegal activity.

What It Pays

Typical starting salaries for customs officers are in the region of £19,587–£25,206 per year.

Prospects

Officers can progress to higher grade posts within the HMRC department.

Best Advice

The HMRC website has some useful case studies of working officers which give a real flavour of this work. You could also get involved in any public service volunteering to gain useful experience, for example through your local police constabulary. Public services diploma courses at further education colleges will also offer insight into the work of a range of public protection services.

Contacts

Her Majesty's Revenue and Customs
www.hmrc.gov.uk

Civil Service Careers
www.careers.civil-service.gov.uk

Runner for Film/TV/Video

You don't need to be an athlete for this job but you will certainly need stamina and energy. This is very much the lowest job on the ladder in film and TV, but is nonetheless a highly sought-after job because it offers one of the best routes into the industry from the ground up. As you might imagine from the name, being a runner is an extremely active and varied role, involving a wide range of tasks including delivering messages and running errands within a production company environment. You might be wondering why someone would want to do this job, but as it is so difficult to break into film or TV this is often the only way to get a first start. Extremely qualified and talented people are prepared to do this often poorly paid (it may even be unpaid) job just to make contacts and get a foot in the door.

The Job Description
Working mainly in production or post-production companies, a runner will deliver equipment, scripts and tapes, collect the film from the processing lab and be a general assistant to anyone who needs help. The runner may pick actors up from the airport/railway station, be sent out to buy particular props, phone round for experts for a film segment, mark up scripts or make the tea. This is an excellent way to build a network of contacts, gain experience of how production works and to understand the film/TV/video industry.

The Person Specification
The job may seem more humdrum than glamorous, but to do it you would need to be:

* extremely motivated to work in the industry
* flexible and able to get on with a wide range of people
* willing to do a variety of different jobs
* able to deal with rejection (you may have to be persistent and present yourself in person for the chance of work)
* ready to do basic administrative/computer work
* able to drive (you may not actually have to run everywhere).

What It Takes
Most runners have taken film/media courses at college or university so that they can speak the right language when applying to companies. A degree in TV or film production may be useful. For university degree study A levels/Diploma and GCSEs at C grade and over, or equivalent, will generally be required. It would be useful to have been involved in film-making as a hobby, through a film club or through a work

placement. Most companies might ask to see examples of your work – a showreel or photos. More than skills or evidence of your talent you will need determination and motivation. You may have to be prepared to do bar or restaurant work at night to be able to afford to work for free as a runner – that's the level of commitment it might take. You might have to work for a year for free or for expenses or on low pay, on various short-term contracts, to gain the experience and credibility to put you in the way of the better work.

What Else

Very few jobs are advertised so you will need to be creative about applying to companies and making them notice you. Research companies through the Producers' Alliance for Cinema and Television (PACT) and be prepared to go in person and ask about possible work. Keep the names of everyone you meet and keep in contact with them – use them as your network of contacts for the future. You will need to be rigorous about networking, making contacts and keeping in touch with them, and be prepared to pester them for future work.

What It Pays

If you are lucky a starting job might pay £10,000 a year, but it might equally pay nothing or just expenses – this may be the only way to get a start in the industry, as being a runner is often a stepping stone to other production work.

Prospects

Most runners have the goal of becoming a director or editor, and this role does give you great experience of all areas of film/TV or video production.

Best Advice

Check out the training programmes offered by FT2 (a national provider of training for freelance careers in film and TV) and CYFLE (a training company for Welsh TV and film). Their funded training programmes (you are paid a training allowance and offered placements with film and TV companies for 12–18 months) are an excellent way of acquiring the skills and experience needed for a range of film and TV careers, including production, sound and editing.

Also look at the Channel 4 Films Talent development scheme (www.channel4.com/4talent), in particular the Summer School 12-week paid placement scheme, and the BBC New Talent schemes (www.bbc.co.uk/newtalent).

Contacts

Broadcasting, Entertainment, Cinematograph and Theatre Union (BECTU),
373–377 Clapham Road, London SW9 9BT
020 7346 0900   www.bectu.org.uk

Skillset, 21 Caledonian Road, London N1 9GB
020 7713 9800   www.skillset.org

PACT
www.pact.co.uk

National Film and Television School
www.nftsfilm-tv.ac.uk

FT2
www.ft2.org.uk

CYFLE
www.cyfle.co.uk

Scriptwriter

Scriptwriters can be writing for TV features or documentaries, for films or theatres or even for adverts. Apart from the specialist writing skills needed, the most important skills necessary to be a good scriptwriter are the ability to be creative and come up with new ideas constantly. As you can imagine, this is a somewhat precarious profession where you are only as good as your last script – many scriptwriters have a more regular day job to keep them solvent while they write and submit scripts to directors/producers.

The Job Description
Scriptwriters write for plays or films and may create a story from scratch or adapt a novel or play into a screenplay. Either way, they need a writing style to suit their material and a creative vision of how this will transfer to the screen or theatre. They have to be able to create a plot and characters that offer a unique way of looking at life, or that simulate real life or a period of history, in an appealing or interesting way. Some scriptwriters will write the commentary or voice-over for a documentary. Most writing involves some kind of research, development of a writing style to suit the subject, creativity to think up a new angle on the subject and the determination and promotion skills to get a director interested in it.

The Person Specification
Scriptwriters might be writing in the hope that they can persuade a director to make that script into reality, or they may be commissioned to write a script for a particular purpose. As most directors/producers like proven talent, it will be hard even to get your scripts read unless you have been published already, you have a good agent or are extremely persuasive in promoting your own work. You will need to be:

- a skilled writer
- creative and talented
- persistent and persuasive
- prepared to take a day job to keep you going, or prepared to have very little money while you are developing your talent.

What It Takes
You could just start writing and sending scripts off to production companies (try Producers Alliance for Cinema and Television – PACT) but some companies discourage unsolicited scripts and it may be difficult to get someone to take notice of your masterpiece. You may need to get yourself a literary agent – check the *Writers' and Artists' Yearbook* at local libraries – who can use contacts to promote your scripts on your behalf.

It is certainly worth making use of the BBC Writer's Room (www.bbc.
co.uk/writersroom) as you can correspond with other writers, read
published scripts and have your own scripts read. The BBC Drama
Writer's Academy also offers courses to develop writers. Channel 4 also
has advice and training schemes which may be useful (www.channel4.
com/4talent).

It is probably worthwhile taking some training in scriptwriting or creative
writing – check local colleges and film/media courses at universities.
In particular look out for courses accredited by Skillset, such as the
Scriptwriting for Film and Television degree course at Bournemouth
University. It is certainly worth considering courses run by the National
Film and Television School and the National Academy of Writing – both
have excellent courses and contacts in the industry.

Most university courses look for at least two or three A levels/Diploma,
or equivalent, and a good GCSE profile with C grades and over. For some
courses you will be asked to send a sample of your writing.

What Else
A creative writing or scriptwriting course is the best way to get feedback
on your writing and style. The National Academy of Writing is a dedicated
writing school that admits students on talent alone and whose patrons
are scriptwriters and authors and poets. They run free events and talks by
successful writers.

What It Pays
This is a mainly freelance occupation so you will be paid according to the
size of the project and your talent and reputation.

Prospects
Many writers have a tough time establishing themselves and some will
have to be extremely motivated to make it. Teaching writing on courses at
colleges might be a parallel career, as is journalism.

Best Advice
Only a small number of the scripts created each year make it into
production, so it is worth researching successful scripts and how they
work – go into cinema or film bookshops or libraries and find out what
makes a good script. Some production companies employ readers to
assess scripts and script ideas – this would be an ideal opportunity to
develop your own critical skills and be in the right place for contacts.
Apply speculatively for reader vacancies at production companies – see
PACT. Do a scriptwriting course at a well-regarded film school – see
Skillset and the Broadcasting, Entertainment, Cinematograph and Theatre
Union (BECTU).

Contacts

Skillset, 21 Caledonian Road, London N1 9GB
020 7713 9800   www.skillset.org

National Academy of Writing, University of Central England
www.thenationalacademyofwriting.org

Broadcasting, Entertainment, Cinematograph and Theatre Union (BECTU),
373–377 Clapham Road, London SW9 9BT
020 7346 0900   www.bectu.org.uk

National Film and Television School
www.nftsfilm-tv.ac.uk

British Film Institute
www.bfi.org.uk

Producers Alliance for Cinema and Television (PACT)
www.pact.co.uk

Scuba Diving Instructor

If you have ever had the chance to scuba dive or snorkel, you might have wondered what it would be like to be an instructor, preferably teaching scuba diving on some idyllic Greek island. For some people, diving is a casual hobby, for others it is a passion. If you feel passionately about it, then the work of diving instructor might suit you. As an instructor, you would be supervising and teaching scuba diving in the UK or abroad.

The Job Description
As a qualified instructor, you will plan and lead diving expeditions, as well as train beginner divers. Speciality instructors can also run specialist training in cavern diving, night diving, underwater photography, wreck diving and multi-level diving. Entry-level diver courses, which instructors would teach, generally cover development of diving skills in a confined space like a swimming pool, performance-based skill tests, and finally some open water dives.

There are various levels of courses that instructors teach, from beginner programmes (Open Water Diver) to Advanced Open Water Diver, Speciality Diver and Rescue Diver. Instructors have to be able to help their pupils enjoy their training, while adhering to strict health and safety guidelines.

The Person Specification
Most people who do this job love diving themselves and want to help others benefit from scuba diving for pleasure or business. Instructors are normally proficient swimmers who are comfortable in the water and who have taken high-level diving courses themselves. They need to be good at explaining to, and dealing with, people, and ready to work in a hands-on way. You will need to be:

- physically fit and a confident swimmer
- able to communicate with people of all ages
- qualified to at least instructor level in scuba diving.

What It Takes
The recognised professional body for scuba diving in the UK and abroad is PADI (Professional Association of Diving Instructors). PADI runs a range of courses from beginner courses in scuba diving to advanced and instructor level. Most instructors start by enjoying scuba diving and by passing Open Water Diving awards. This is normally followed by Advanced Open Water Diving training and possibly Medic First Aid.

Rescue Diver training comes next and this leads onto the first level of instructor training, known as the Divemaster qualification. Following this, assistant instructor training starts, leading to instructor development courses and exams.

At Advanced Open Water diving level, you would get the chance to try out a number of specialisms like boat, drift, multi-level or wreck diving, but for more in-depth specialisation you might take the PADI speciality diver courses. The Rescue Diver course qualifies you to ensure dives are safe and to prevent potential accidents.

Divemaster qualifies you to organise and supervise diving activities and the course covers watermanship and stamina, diving skills, diving physiology, dive planning and training.

PADI courses are privately run, at different costs, by different dive centres and some colleges. Some colleges can subsidise costs for the unemployed.

What Else
Costs for PADI courses vary, so it is worth comparing prices at a range of PADI centres. Many people take their first PADI courses abroad as part of a holiday.

What It Pays
This is very difficult to say, as it depends whether the work is in the UK or abroad and what level of diver education you have achieved. Work may be seasonal, from contract to contract, and may offer accommodation at your diver centre. It is possible that you could earn between £50 and £110 per day as an instructor but check diver job websites for more information on this – for example the PADI site and Flying Fish (www.flyingfishonline.com).

Prospects
Job opportunities for instructors seem to be increasing as more people want to learn to dive, particularly in diving centres abroad.

Best Advice
Try out diving for fun first and then decide if you want to take it further.

Contacts
PADI International Ltd, Unit 7, St Phillips Central, Albert Road, St Phillips, Bristol BS2 0PD
0117 300 7234   www.padi.com

Skin Camouflage Technician

For all sorts of reasons, people may have skin conditions for which some kind of camouflage treatment might be helpful. As a result of scarring, an accident, a birthmark or injury of some kind, someone might seek help to mask a minor or significant disfigurement. As you can imagine, the technician who helps with this can often help someone both physically and mentally, with the right kind of treatment often substantially improving someone's life.

The Job Description

Camouflage technicians teach people how to use specialist creams and techniques to achieve as near as possible a restoration of appearance, and concealment of hyperpigmented or scarred skin. They deal with a range of conditions such as reddened skin, skin which has lost pigment, unwanted tattoos, burns, scars and birthmarks. The transformation for patients can be life changing and the psychological benefits are proven. Technicians are skilled in make-up techniques and have a knowledge of the range of products, creams and covering powders that will best match the skin colour. They instruct patients in the best techniques so that they can be self-sufficient and confident about using the techniques themselves after leaving hospital.

The Person Specification

Technicians must be able to interact with people, putting them at their ease and giving them confidence that the techniques and products used will work to disguise skin imperfections. You would need to have:

- a sensitive and caring disposition, with a positive, proactive manner
- an ability to be gentle with your hands
- good colour-matching awareness
- a creative, practical approach
- an awareness of medical conditions that cause skin imperfections
- an interest in encouraging people to learn the skills themselves.

What It Takes

There are a number of ways to train for this; some people train through make-up courses run by colleges as part of a beauty therapy or holistic therapy course, or even through theatrical media make-up courses. The courses may be BTEC or City & Guilds courses, and normally GCSE level or equivalent in 2–3 subjects (ideally at C grade and over, or equivalent) is needed for entry to these courses. Alternatively you could train as a volunteer with the British Red Cross as a skin camouflage volunteer, based in an NHS hospital. The British Red Cross recruits volunteers who have good interpersonal skills and an excellent eye for colour and tone, and puts them through a five-day training course. Also, the British Association of Skin Camouflage offers four-day workshop courses to train people who have make-up experience through beauty therapy courses or through NHS work.

What Else
The NHS recruits technicians or health-care assistants for this work but private hospitals or even overseas charities in war or disaster zones might also be interested in people with these important skills.

What It Pays
NHS pay rates start at £12,577–£15,523 per year.

Prospects
Various health or social care careers could be open to you if you train for this work, and research into dermatology or work with cosmetics companies could be a possible future career prospect.

Best Advice
Volunteer and be trained through the British Red Cross – this would be ideal experience.

Contacts
British Association of Skin Camouflage, PO Box 202, Macclesfield SK11 6FP
01625 871129   www.skin-camouflage.net

Red Cross
www.redcross.org

NHS Careers
www.nhscareers.nhs.uk

Snowboard Instructor

If you are a keen snowboarder you may be self-taught or have had some initial lessons from an instructor. Instructors ensure that snowboarders have the techniques and confidence to enjoy this exciting sport. As with most sports instruction, snowboard instructors firstly have to be extremely proficient at snowboarding before they can train to instruct others.

The Job Description

Snowboard instructors have a thorough grounding in the practice of snowboarding and an ability to plan lessons for both the practical on-snow aspects, and the theory and health and safety aspects of the role. They will work for approved centres teaching on different levels of courses in particular ski-controlled areas. You could be dealing with a range of students, of differing abilities, including those who are proficient skiers but new to snowboarding and those who have never skied or snowboarded before.

The Person Specification

Adventure sports instructors are often enthusiasts at their sports and may have developed a natural ability. Typical students may be less able to learn quickly and may need encouragement and support to develop the skills needed. You will need to be:

- patient and a good communicator
- able to assess confidence and encourage students
- organised and able to plan lesson segments to keep students interested
- committed to health and safety
- enthusiastic about snowboarding and able to demonstrate techniques in a clear way.

What It Takes

To be a licensed instructor you will need to take British Association of Snowsports Instructors (BASI) qualification Level 1 at the very least. Level 1 allows you to instruct in the UK only on a dry slope or a controlled snow slope environment. To work abroad you will need a Level 1 and Level 2 BASI qualification and a first-aid qualification (taken over a minimum of 12 hours). Once qualified to Level 2 you are a fully qualified BASI member.

To get on a Level 1 trainee instructor course you will need to be a confident and competent snowboarder who can do red runs, small radius turns at a steady pace and black runs in full control. Typically trainee instructors will have at least 16 weeks of experience as a recreational snowboarder. Level 1 courses can be five-day on-snow courses or longer, depending on the snowboard school. Level 2 courses may be 10-day on-snow courses, with evening lectures for theory and a written exam paper. These courses are generally costly so do your research – expect to pay in the region of £5,000, which might include accommodation, insurance, ski passes etc.

Courses involve the technical stages of snowboarding and how to teach, as well as safety and fitness for snowboarding.

After the Level 1 course you will need to gain 35 hours of ski school experience before you can go onto the Level 2 course to qualify as a fully licensed instructor.

What Else
There are many ski/snowboard companies that offer training for instructor qualifications and possible employment once qualified. Make sure the training offered is BASI accredited.

What It Pays
Many people do this job for love and because it allows them to get out on the slopes themselves. Pay sometimes includes accommodation, perhaps €1,000 a month in Europe, or in the region of £10,000–£15,000 per year. The work is often seasonal and contracts are often offered on a seasonal basis.

Prospects
It is possible to ski all the year round, following the snow, as an instructor. You might then progress to train on the instructor courses (train new instructors) with BASI accredited companies.

Best Advice
Get lots of snow experience and budget carefully to be able to pay for your instructor training.

Contacts
British Association of Snowsports Instructors (BASI), Glenmore, Aviemore PH22 1QU
01479 861 717   www.basi.org.uk

The Institute for Outdoor Learning
www.outdoor-learning.org

Sommelier

A sommelier is an experienced wine waiter who is an expert at creating a wine list and recommending wines to restaurant customers. Their job involves much more than what you see as they have the full responsibility for managing the process of wine buying and selection for licensed premises. They have to be able to taste wine to check its quality and know how to keep wine in the best condition. They control all stock and deliveries, and train other staff in wine service.

The Job Description
The sommelier will liaise with the chef to decide wines to be recommended for certain menu items, and the wine list will be created by him/her. They are responsible for the purchase of wines and will ensure that wines are conserved in the right way. They may create a cocktail menu and will certainly be on hand to make recommendations about wines. They need to use their expertise to help customers select wines and may work with wedding or conference planners to suggest wine choices, according to menu options. Sommeliers also serve wine at the table or in bars.

The Person Specification
To do this job, you would be someone with a passionate interest in wine, its history and production. You would also need to be customer focused and keen to help diners make the best wine choices according to their budget. For this job you would need to have:

- a discerning sense of taste
- an ability to interact well with people
- commitment to learning about wine
- a willingness to work unsocial hours in an active job.

What It Takes
Most people train for this work through hospitality and catering apprenticeships or college courses. As a trainee waiter you could take NVQs in hospitality at Levels 2 and 3 and then take further wine education courses through the Wine and Spirit Education Trust. For entry to apprenticeships and/or NVQ courses a good GCSE profile or equivalent, with English and maths (ideally D grade and over) is required.

The University of Brighton (www.brighton.ac.uk) offers some unusual wine courses such as their Foundation degrees in Wine Business or Wine Production which offer training in wine analysis and placements on UK vineyards. For these courses GCSE or equivalent in maths, English and science at C grade or above (or equivalent) and one A Level/Diploma or equivalent are required.

What Else

Sommeliers may work for small or large restaurants or wine bars or hospitality/hotel chains and will probably wear a particular uniform to denote their role.

What It Pays

Starting salaries for a trainee sommelier are in the range £12,000–£13,000 per year.

Prospects

As head or chief sommelier, earnings can be in the region of £45,000 per year and travel abroad to tastings can be possible.

Best Advice

Cultivate your palate by learning about wine and by attending tasting sessions for different varieties of wines. Check the Wine and Spirit Education Trust (WSET) website for courses.

Contacts

Wine and Spirit Education Trust (WSET), 39–45 Bermondsey Street, London SE1 3XF
0207 089 3845   www.wset.co.uk

Brighton University Wine Studies courses
www.brighton.ac.uk

Sound Engineer

This job can mean a lot of different things but, essentially, this is about producing sound mixes for TV/radio/theatre, or for music production and the recording, editing and mixing that produce the eventual sound, broadcast, music or recording. Sound engineers can work in recording studios or as a sound technician in the theatre, or even as a radio studio manager for a radio station.

The Job Description

Sound engineers are responsible for the technical quality of the sound they produce, using their skills and knowledge to create and transmit sound using manual, digital and computerised techniques. They could work in acoustics for companies that produce music equipment, or for music companies that produce the music that you listen to on the radio or on your CD player. In radio or TV their specialist skills are used to record and mix sound and then, in post-production, to create the perfect track. On a film or TV set they might be operating the boom microphone to record the voice action on set, or rigging equipment; post-production they might be perfecting the sound quality and/or adding sound effects. For a radio programme they will be supervising the transmission, organising phone-ins, setting up outside broadcasts and checking the sound quality of the presenters' or guests' voices (sound checks).

The Person Specification

This work is suited to people who are fascinated by sound and how it is produced, and who have an extremely good ear in order to pick up crackling on a tape or distortion in a recording. For this work you would need to be:

- enthusiastic about music and sound with a good ear for sound quality
- interested in the technical side of how sound is produced and transmitted
- willing to train and learn the skills of recording and mixing
- determined to make a career in a competitive, often insecure profession
- good with computers and with an interest in electronics and digital media.

What It Takes

Some people move into this work from an electronics background (having trained after GCSEs or equivalent through an apprenticeship in electronics) or after DJ work as a hobby. Some do volunteer work in hospital radio (www.hospitalradio.co.uk) and learn the skills they need there. There are many good sound engineering/recording/music technology courses on offer at various universities, some offering placements in the industry. Some, like the course at Salford University in acoustics, audio and video, offer training in designing recording studios,

and developing mixing consoles and PA systems. Check www.ucas.com
to find Foundation and degree courses in sound/recording engineering and
broadcast technologies, searching under sound and acoustics headings.

Other courses on offer are theatre sound courses such as that offered by
the Central School of Speech and Drama, the Sound Technology course
at the Liverpool Institute of the Performing Arts (LIPA) and the Sound,
Light and Live Event Technology course at the University of Derby. Many
courses will expect you to have A levels/Diploma or equivalent, possibly
including maths and/or physics, or the Music Technology BTEC Diploma,
as well as a GCSE profile at C grade and above or equivalent.

What Else

Recording studios tend to be dark and windowless; the hours of work
can be long and unsocial. Competition for jobs is fierce. Vacancies are not
always advertised so make your own contacts in the industry so that you
have a network of friends who will recommend you for work or let you
know of upcoming possibilities. Try to gain work experience of any kind
through the BBC Work Experience scheme or through a local recording
studio. Get familiar with recording software. Persistence and technical
skills will be the key to gaining work.

What It Pays

Typical starting salaries can be around £10,000–£16,000 per year.
Freelancers can earn approximately £500 per week.

Prospects

Sound engineers can move into many different areas of work and can
progress to radio producer or video/film/TV producer work with experience.

Best Advice

Get any experience you can with hospital radio and/or local radio
stations. Check out training schemes at the BBC and through FT2, a
training scheme which offers paid training as a sound assistant. The Radio
Academy website has a good section called 'Getting into Radio'.

Contacts

Skillset, 21 Caledonian Road, London N1 9GB
020 7713 9800 www.skillset.org

BBC Recruitment
www.bbc.co.uk/jobs

FT2
www.FT2.org.uk

The Radio Academy
www.radioacademy.org

Sports Development Officer

If the idea of a job connected to sport seems the perfect career to you, it may be worth considering the role of sports development officer. A sports development officer is involved in the promotion of sport for all ages within an area; this includes facilitating new sporting programmes and liaising with national and local sporting and coaching bodies.

The Job Description

The main responsibility of a sports development officer (SDO) is to promote sport by encouraging people to participate in sporting activities. This is done by organising and setting up programmes for local people to get involved in sport at any level. SDOs help develop coaching courses and use a network of community contacts to motivate local people to participate in sport and recreation.

While the job is essentially office based, an SDO spends a great deal of time out and about meeting the local community, liaising with sport and leisure centres, and national and local sporting bodies. Often, they may have a special responsibility to tempt people who have never been sporty to try sport and find one that suits.

The Person Specification

SDOs spend their time making contacts at a local level and offering help to attract funding for different sporting projects. They may also assist community groups in finding funding for facilities, or they may set up and run summer sports camps for young people, as well as offering training for coaches. Some may act as active sports coordinators with a role to encourage participation in specific sports.

Some SDOs work for a particular sporting body such as the Netball Association or the Rugby Football Union, for example, and they may have a geographical area of the country as their responsibility. They would work with clubs, offering support to run events, promote coaching, market the sport and encourage participation through schools and the local community. For this work, you would need to be:

- committed to encouraging sport and recreation in the community
- outgoing and confident with excellent interpersonal skills
- a good communicator and persuader
- organised and flexible.

What It Takes

Most people who apply for these jobs have a degree, Foundation degree, or equivalent, in sports science/studies or similar, so taking a course of university-level study in these areas is valuable. Some applicants have only BTEC/A level/Diploma in sport or PE but may gain entry to this work with substantial, relevant experience – for example coaching experience or volunteer community sports leader work.

Useful additional qualifications are national coaching awards for a number of sporting bodies and the community sports leader award, which is available at many local colleges on a part-time or full-time basis.

Voluntary work in any sporting or community context is valuable, along with evidence, by way of references, as to your personal suitability for this work.

Work for a national sporting body may require you to have competed at a high level in sport yourself.

What Else

There are a lot of good applicants for these posts when they are advertised, so you will need to promote yourself well in your application. Coaching qualifications, community language skills or deaf signing or youth work experience would all be valuable in making you look a stronger applicant. You will probably need Criminal Records Bureau (CRB) clearance for this work.

What It Pays

Pay rates vary across the country, but starting salaries in general can be around £13,700–£18,700 per year for local government posts and slightly higher, at about £16,000–£22,000 per year, for work with sporting bodies/associations.

Prospects

Sport and the sports development industry is one of the fastest-growing industries at the moment, so job opportunities are increasing, but there are a great number of sport-related courses at universities, so competition is fierce for jobs.

Jobs can be with local county, borough or city councils or with sport governing bodies; for example the RFU (Rugby Football Union) might advertise sports development officer posts across the country to promote rugby in schools and clubs.

Jobs are advertised in national and local newspapers, on the Institute for Sport, Parks and Leisure (ISPAL) website and on the UK Sport site.

Best Advice

Aim to gain high-level academic qualifications in sport through a university-level course and supplement this with coaching awards, community sports leader awards and sport-related voluntary work in the community such as on sport camps and play schemes. Vacation work on sports camps in Europe, USA, Australia and Canada may also be useful, as might gap-year sports work in developing countries.

Contacts

UK Sport, 40 Bernard Street, London WC1N 1ST
020 7211 5100   www.uksport.gov.uk

Institute for Sport, Parks and Leisure (ISPAL)
www.ispal.org.uk

Sports Journalist

Sports journalists can work for the print media (newspapers) or TV and radio, and are responsible for reporting and writing about sporting events, which might be national, regional or often local. They have to be enthusiastic about sport in general, but probably specialise in one or two particular sports. They have to be knowledgeable about these particular sports and able to communicate this in writing, on TV or on the radio in a compelling, interesting way. Increasingly, they may even write for internet-based magazines or the interactive, digital media. While the job may sound very exciting, the reality of journalism is more likely to be long hours and hard work, watching a minor league football match rather than hanging out with your favourite team's players.

The Job Description

This can vary according to the area of specialism. Print journalists collect information by telephone or by personal interviews, recording the information using shorthand. They may attend sporting events and take notes to capture the experience of being there. They may try to interview players or managers of a local team to make a good story. Once they have sufficient information, they write the story in an interesting way, using a computer or laptop at the event/game. Broadcast journalists have to follow leads about possible stories, going to sporting events with a technical and camera crew and interviewing key people. They may conduct a pre-recorded interview or do it live 'on air'. Remember that this might be at a local school tournament or at a minor league club. Other journalists might work in the sports newsroom and write news bulletins and edit news tapes from other journalists.

The Person Specification

Sports reporters have to be adaptable and be able to communicate information in an interesting and concise way. Accurate, concise writing has more impact, and so being able to write rambling, creative essays at school is unlikely to be useful or relevant for this work. You would need to be:

- persistent and good at research
- almost obsessive about sport, the statistics, the names of the players, with a good memory and overall knowledge
- good at dealing with people
- good at noticing detail
- resourceful and able to use your initiative
- prepared to work irregular hours
- able to customise your writing to the potential reader or audience

• articulate – gifted with words and with an expressive voice, if you are going for broadcast journalism.

What It Takes
Most journalists today have degrees, which might be in journalism, media or any subject that develops writing and research skills. Typically, graduates of journalism degrees may enter local newspapers as trainees, dealing with a variety of news and local interest stories, and after further experience begin to specialise in sports events and/or move into local radio reporting and onto TV. This is by no means an easy route and competition at all levels is intense. Degree holders of other subjects may gain trainee places on newspapers or on TV graduate training schemes or they may take a one-year postgraduate qualification in journalism.

All journalism courses that are worth taking are generally accredited by the National Council for the Training of Journalists (NCTJ) or the Broadcast Journalism Training Council (BJTC). There are other shorter, more intensive courses also available – check with the NCTJ and BJTC for good course information. The universities of Brighton and Sunderland have specialist sports journalism courses, accredited by the NCTJ.

For those not wanting to take a degree, there are still one-year pre-entry to journalism courses available (A levels/Diploma required), which can lead to trainee posts with a further two years' training on a newspaper.

There are also some broadcast journalism courses (mainly postgraduate level) recommended by the BJTC; these tend to focus on radio journalism, which might allow progression into TV work.

Whatever course you apply for, A levels/Diploma, or equivalent, plus good GCSE passes at C grade and over, including English, will probably be required. Postgraduate courses will require degree-level qualifications, but all prospective applicants will be expected to show good writing skills and possibly some student writing experience.

What Else
In addition to sporting knowledge, sports journalists have to be good at spelling, using IT and working to deadlines. An understanding of the law of libel may also be considered a good additional extra and is normally covered on journalism courses.

What It Pays
Trainees may start on £12,000–£13,000 a year on local newspapers, and broadcast journalists may start on £15,000–£18,000 per year.

Prospects
Career progression is through experience and reputation as a writer/broadcaster.

Best Advice

Take media-related courses at college level that develop writing and editing skills. Write for a student newspaper and practise debating as part of a group. Talk to a journalist to find out what the job is really like and, ideally, get some work experience.

For radio work, try and do some hospital radio work (www.hospitalradio. co.uk). Try sending your own match reports to local newspapers.

Contacts

National College for the Training of Journalists (NCTJ), The New Granary, Station Road, Newport, Saffron Walden, Essex CB11 3PL
01799 544014   www.nctj.com

Broadcast Journalism Training Council (BJTC), 18 Millers Close, Rippingale, Near Bourne, Lincolnshire PE10 0TH
01778 440025   www.bjtc.org.uk

Hold The Front Page
www.holdthefrontpage.co.uk

Sports Psychologist

This is a specialist area of sports science and involves supporting sports professionals in order to help them achieve their best performance through awareness of their own motivation, thinking and behaviour triggers, and how these factors might help or hinder their actual potential. Even with the most skilled and dedicated sportsperson who trains to the highest level physically, it is now recognised that the psychological/ motivational component can be enormously important. Research into this area of supporting athletes' preparation has shown that the work of sports psychologists can be extremely beneficial in enhancing or increasing performance.

The Job Description

While much of the focus is on improvement of sporting performance through psychological treatment or therapy methods, sports psychologists also research the benefits of sport for someone's psychological health, so the range of the work involved can be extremely varied and is constantly developing. For example, current government initiatives to encourage sport in deprived communities (sport development officer roles) are based on research that sport can work to diffuse tension and aggression while promoting positive feelings and experiences.

As a general rule, sports psychologists work in two main areas; they can work for sporting organisations like the Sports Council or sports clubs or governing bodies/associations, or with specialist charities (such as disability support charities), helping athletes motivate themselves through understanding their own typical patterns or focusing on specific aspects of their training. Alternatively, they might work in universities with a strong sporting reputation doing research into specific sports psychology issues and offering consultancy to sports organisations, clubs and charities.

The Person Specification

This work requires an interesting and varied mix of skills and abilities. Sports psychologists have to be interested in people and the sporting talent they have, and be able to suggest techniques to improve their mental preparation. They might suggest visualisation or relaxation techniques, or they may encourage more awareness of negative thoughts, which might act as a mental stumbling block to their 'psyching up' for an event. They also have to be interested in research into what affects performance and how sport can be used to promote physical and mental health, not just for talented sportspeople, but for the community at large. To do this work, you would have to be:

- committed to the idea of the benefits of sport
- interested in sport and even a keen sportsperson yourself
- a good communicator and counsellor for sportspeople encountering performance problems
- able to work with other professionals, including coaches and physiotherapists
- able to use scientific principles to analyse problems with sporting performance
- interested in the science of exercise and fitness
- logical and methodical for research work.

What It Takes

There is no one way into this work, but some kind of degree course and postgraduate study is usual in subjects such as sport, exercise science and psychology, probably as a combined course. You will need a degree course that has a substantial psychology component – enough to attain the Graduate Basis for Registration (GBR) through the British Psychological Society. Once you have GBR you would continue your training through postgraduate study in sport and exercise psychology. The British Association of Sport and Exercise Sciences (BASES) accredits sports psychologists and sports scientists so check the BASES site and www.ucas.com for further information on suitable degree courses, which would be your starting point. What is important is that you need to have a scientific approach to this work, so good GCSEs or equivalent with C grades and above and A levels/Diploma or equivalent in sciences such as biology and chemistry are important for higher-level study.

What Else

This career is still relatively new in the UK, but is well developed in the USA and Australia. Competition for posts with top clubs and national sporting organisations is intense, so be sure that you can gain the best qualifications and experience.

What It Pays

Consultancy or freelance work is common, so pay rates are difficult to gauge. Universities and national organisations offer good starting salaries – around £25,000 per year and upwards, depending on experience and qualifications.

Prospects

As this is a developing career, possibilities can be wide ranging. If you can help an international sportsperson overcome a mental block, you could find yourself with great earnings and a high job-satisfaction level.

Best Advice

Get involved in sport, play competitively, gain coaching qualifications and work for free for sports clubs to gain experience. Work hard at subjects such as biology, chemistry and psychology.

Contacts

The British Association of Sport and Exercise Sciences, 114 Cardigan Road, Headingley, Leeds LS6 3BJ
0113 230 7558   www.bases.org.uk

UK Sport, 40 Bernard Street, London WC1N 1ST
020 7211 5100   www.uksport.gov.uk

Stunt Artist

Action films and death-defying stunts – most of us have an idea about stunt work, but it takes incredible sporting skill and expertise, agility and lengthy, often expensive, training to do this kind of work.

The Job Description

Stunt performers act as stand-ins on film and TV sets for the actors in any scene that might include a dangerous or risky element. The skill of the stunt performer is to perform a stunt that is technical, exciting and often risky, and make it look easy.

Most stunt performers specialise in particular stunts such as high falls, fights, stair falls, horseriding, skiing, parachuting, high diving, swimming or scuba diving, motorcycle or precision driving work, or even BMX riding or wheelchair wheelies.

They may arrange as well as perform their own stunts – this can involve painstaking planning and analysis of what will work and have the most impact. They have to work long hours on film and TV sets, often starting in make-up at 4a.m. and being part of filming from 7.30a.m. onwards. They have to coordinate with film or TV technicians, producers and staff to plan the stunt component of the film or programme. They plan every detail and practise moves until they are sure that the performance will be convincing. Every proposed stunt has to be checked for health and safety risks to the performers.

The Person Specification

Successful stunt performers have a number of key skills and abilities, which must include an ongoing commitment to staying fit so that they are always in good shape to do the job. You would need to be:

- confident and outgoing
- interested in sport with proven skill qualifications in at least six areas from skiing, fencing, gymnastics, boxing, martial arts, parachuting, diving, climbing, motorbike riding, horseriding, swimming, rock-climbing, mountaineering etc.
- prepared and keen to perform, preferably with some acting experience, even in an amateur way
- able to cope with working in an insecure job with high risk factors.

What It Takes

To work as a stunt performer in the UK, you need to be accepted by the British Equity Stunt Register and the Joint Industry Stunt Committee (JISC). The JISC register means you would start out as a probationary member for at least three years, compiling a log book of work done under the supervision of a stunt/action coordinator. After three years of experience you may then progress to being an intermediate member, then a full member of JISC. You would have to be aged 18 or over to apply to join this register.

Certain approved qualifications have to be passed in at least six specific sporting and skill areas – these are laid down by British Equity: www. equity.org.uk. You would have to take and pass relevant training courses at the recommended levels in these six separate sports or skills, and you would have to renew your competency level on a regular basis. Normally at least one year's experience and qualifications in each skill are required.

It costs a great deal to complete the recommended training and gain the accepted qualifications for stunt performing. The average cost for training may be in the region of £10,000–£20,000. Trainee performers have to fund this themselves. They also have to be an Equity member and be in excellent health, with a medical report to prove this.

What Else

This is a dangerous, insecure profession. Many performers experience periods of unemployment or work on a contract-to-contract basis. Advances in digital photography, computer graphics and special effects have meant that certain stunts can be created and enhanced without the use of stunt performers, meaning potentially less work for stunt artists.

What It Pays

It is difficult to work out a typical stunt performer's earnings due to the irregular nature of the work. Pay rates are set by Equity and may be in the region of £390–£500 per day, but this is dependent on the stunt or action sequence and what is required. Most stunt performers are self-employed, and are paid a fee for each job.

Prospects

There may only be about 300 stunt performers in the UK and industry sources suggest that only about 100 are in regular work. Competition for work is intense and spells of unemployment are not unusual. Second-income jobs for stunt performers are common.

Some performers move into stunt arrangement or co-ordination jobs on film or TV sets, or into work as the second unit director on the action sequences of films or TV programmes.

Best Advice

Only think about doing this work if you are totally motivated and willing to commit yourself to a lengthy, expensive training. It may be possible to gain valuable experience in stunt-related work at theme parks, acting out medieval jousts or battles. Take your own health and fitness seriously and aim to reach the highest standards in your chosen areas of expertise. Aim to get some substantial experience on film or TV sets as an extra or for walk-on parts.

Contacts

Try reading *Variety* and *The Stage* magazines for a good general background to the entertainment industry.

Skillset, 21 Caledonian Road, London N1 9GB
020 7713 9800   www.skillset.org

JISC, JIGS Ltd c/o BECTU (Broadcasting, Entertainment, Cinematograph and Theatre Union)
www.bectu.org.uk

Subtitler

Subtitling involves presenting the entire soundtrack, or an abbreviated version of the soundtrack, of a TV programme or film in a text format so that it can be viewed on screen. This is done mainly for deaf and hard-of-hearing viewers or for foreign-language films. The accuracy with which the text represents the programme or film is crucial. The job can involve simply producing a verbatim transcript or an edited version that retains the meaning and the liveliness of the original. Most of the subtitling work is done in post-production (after the film or programme is made) but there are occasions when real-time or live subtitles are needed; this is increasingly used for live sports programmes, using voice recognition software.

The Job Description

Subtitlers work for film or TV companies, interpreting the sound aspect of the programme or film, editing it where necessary and transposing it into clear, easy-to-read subtitles, which, as the BBC says, 'retain the full sense and flavour of the programme'. They have to write subtitles over a range of programmes and topics, often working to very tight deadlines to produce text. They have to check and alter their work for accuracy and be able to convey often complex ideas or sounds through clear and concise language. They are not just typists, but skilled writers and editors who have to convey all the excitement and drama. This may involve transposing conversations and sound effects, describing moves or even relaying emotions. In some ways they are like a narrator who describes a story or programme in abbreviated but intense detail.

The Person Specification

Subtitlers need strong editing and English-language skills, with perfect spelling and grammar and a natural gift for punctuation. Live subtitlers have to be able to produce live commentary, which is turned instantly into subtitles through voice recognition software (known as 'respeaking'). For this work you would need to be:

- able to understand and analyse complex information and transpose it into clear, informative subtitles
- aware of the difficulties that hearing-impaired people face when watching TV
- confident using technology and computers
- interested in the media and the world around you
- able to work efficiently and accurately as part of a team
- able to work to tight deadlines and under pressure.

What It Takes

Subtitlers can be trained on the job in the use of specialist software, as long as they have the language and editing skills required. Degrees or even Master's-level study in publishing, English language or linguistics might be useful to persuade an employer of your suitability for this work. You will need A levels/Diploma or equivalent and a good GCSE (or equivalent) profile with C grades and above for entry to university-level courses. There is an MA in Monolingual Subtitling and Audio Description at the University of Surrey which offers specialist training for this work. Often you will be expected to undergo a practical test in editing or 'respeaking' for voice recognition software at interview to check if you have the relevant potential.

For foreign-language or interlingual subtitling, you would need to have an excellent vocabulary and complete fluency in at least one other language (other than your own first language), normally to degree standard as a starting point. Then you would need either to study at Master's level for an MA in translation studies, or gain a trainee position in a film subtitling company. Most translation courses have a module which covers subtitling – see courses at Imperial College London, the University of Sheffield or Roehampton University for examples.

What Else

The BBC often advertises subtitling jobs in its online jobs section, while companies such as the Independent Media Support Group (www.ims-media.com) regularly advertise for trainee live subtitlers. Many jobs are in London but there are specialist companies in Europe too.

What It Pays

Starting salary in London could be around £20,000 per year, but pay rates are variable according to the nature of the work.

Prospects

Subtitlers can also work for film companies in post-production to make foreign films accessible to all filmgoers. This kind of work also involves foreign-language translation skills.

Best Advice

Develop grammar, spelling and English-language skills. Visit the Plain English site and consider courses in writing clear and direct language – www.plainenglish.co.uk.

Contacts

Skillset, 21 Caledonian Road, London N1 9GB
020 7713 9800   www.skillset.org

BBC
www.bbc.co.uk/jobs or www.bbc.co.uk/workexperience

The Subtitlers' Association
www.subtitler.org.uk

The European Association for Studies in Screen Translation (ESIST)
www.esist.org

Tea Taster

With over 1,500 different types of tea being produced, there is considerably more to being a tea taster than just liking tea. The tea taster has to use more than just their sense of taste. They will also use smell, sight and touch to evaluate and judge tea samples so that they can grade and bid for tea from different producers, deciding on quality and price value so that tea can be bought and supplied to supermarkets and specialist tea shops throughout the country. In essence, the tea buyer and taster are one and the same role, and this work has much in common with that of wine buyer/tasters.

The Job Description

The tea taster/buyer has to do more than just taste teas. They have to take into account the quality of blends, ensuring consistency of taste for leading well-known brands. They also have to be knowledgeable about weather and growing conditions for tea, exchange rates, world consumption, supply and demand, and other key economic or political factors. It is the job of the tea taster to be an expert on the qualities of teas from different estates, the value of teas, the blends, the production process, and the purchasing/buying function according to market rates and seasonal quality.

The Person Specification

A trained tea taster might be sampling between 400 and 1,000 teas a day and the process by which this is done is much like a tea ritual, with strict rules to ensure proper tasting conditions. Typically, the tea taster will examine the dry leaf first for quality, colour and texture. Then boiling water will be added to the leaves and the leaves left to infuse for five to six minutes. Then the taster will examine the wet leaves very carefully for colour and aroma. Finally, the taster will 'slurp' (a technical term) the tea, allowing it to hit the back of the palate at a speed so that the full power of the tea can be experienced.

This is only one part of the job, as the buyer role also includes dealing with market reports and price forecasts, appointing agents at tea auctions and assessing markets for best-quality products according to seasonal information. For this work, you would need to be:

- very aware of your senses, in particular taste, smell and sight
- fascinated by the history and production of tea
- able to pay attention to detail and take account of economic and political factors
- committed to creating a high-quality product with consistency.

What It Takes

On average, it takes about five years to train as a tea taster as this is how long it takes to develop your taste buds to the right level of discernment. For the first 12–18 months, a trainee spends up to 30 hours a week tasting tea from different estates and doing 'blind' testing to develop their senses. After this period, trainees are often sent overseas to producing countries to develop their tea knowledge.

Most tea tasters start as graduate trainees with large food companies, such as Tetley's or Taylors of Harrogate, who are in the business of tea production and distribution. They may have taken food science or technology-related degrees, or possibly scientific degrees, such as chemistry. You will need to have an all-round GCSE (or equivalent) education and A levels/Diploma, or equivalent, for degree-level study. It may be possible to move into tasting from food company laboratory work without university study, but as there are limited jobs in this area, university study of some kind is recommended.

What Else

The tea that is bought has to reach the supermarket shelf within 20–30 weeks of being plucked for optimum freshness, so tea tasting and buying are ongoing to ensure a constant supply. Travel overseas is a constant part of this work. Being a busy tea taster can result in stained teeth so teeth brushing and hygiene might be a priority.

What It Pays

Salaries for graduate trainee schemes start at around £23,000 per year.

Prospects

Some teas are blended from as many as 35 different teas and tea tasters can move into blending work or into senior buyer roles.

Best Advice

Do your research into the tea-growing industry and start tasting different types of tea (in leaf not bag form) to develop your taste buds. Vacation experience with one of the large tea-production companies or sandwich course experience through a food science degree might be possible and would be valuable. Check out the websites in the contacts section below.

Contacts

Taylors of Harrogate, Plumpton Park, Harrogate HG2 7LD
01423 814000   www.taylorsofharrogate.co.uk

Jacksons of Piccadilly
www.jacksonsofpiccadilly.co.uk

Tetley Ltd
www.tetley.co.uk

United Kingdom Tea Council
www.tea.co.uk

Teaching English as a Foreign Language

Being a teacher of English as a foreign language (TEFL) means that you can work overseas or in this country helping foreign students to learn English. This is sometimes also referred to as Teaching English as a Second Language (TESOL), which in many ways is a more accurate description of the work, as many people wish to learn English as a second language for business, leisure or educational/career purposes. It may be that you would be teaching business people, students or young people in a number of uses of English, but the main emphasis is on helping them to become confident conversationally. Typically, this could mean that you might be working in countries like Japan or Spain for the British Council, in language schools abroad, or be based in the UK teaching refugees, asylum seekers, foreign visitors or students, all of whom wish to learn English for a variety of reasons.

The Job Description
TEFL teachers can teach on short courses for conversational English or on more in-depth courses for business people. There is no requirement to speak the language of the TEFL students, as English is spoken all the time. A variety of teaching methods are used, including role plays, group and individual work. Audio-visual materials might be used as well. Teachers have to be sensitive and sympathetic to the wide range of cultures of their students and customise the lessons to the students' particular needs; this might involve, for example, the use of business terminology for business students or specific legal or medical terminology for other students.

The Person Specification
The main skill in this work is an ability to explain ideas and information clearly and present lesson exercises in an interesting way. Ability levels within a group can vary, so the teacher needs to pace activities accordingly. You would need to be:

- patient and persevering
- a good communicator
- committed to helping people learn
- interested in other countries and other cultures
- interested in English and in other languages too.

What It Takes
The two most widely recognised qualifications for this work are the Cambridge Certificate/Diploma in English Language Teaching to Adults (CELTA/DELTA) and the Trinity College London Certificate in Teaching

English to Speakers of Other Languages (TESOL). These courses are offered at various centres and colleges around the country and can last from four weeks (intensive) to one year, depending on whether they are studied full or part time. Most people study these courses to gain qualifications which are accepted by language schools abroad.

For these courses, degree-level or at least A level/Diploma (or equivalent) qualifications are normally needed. A good standard of English, including grammar, is vital. Some teacher training courses (for teaching in UK schools and colleges) offer a TEFL qualification as an extra. For work in colleges in the UK, you would need both a TEFL/TESOL qualification and a full teaching qualification.

What Else
Work overseas can be found through the British Council. In the UK, work can be with private language schools, adult education centres or colleges, but it may be seasonal (summer temporary work) to fit in with foreign visitors or students.

What It Pays
Pay rates range from £15,000–£23,000 per year for new TEFL teachers.

Prospects
There is a constant and increasing demand for English-language teaching, so job opportunities are good.

Best Advice
There are good information sources and links to qualifications on the British Council website. A good TEFL qualification opens up job opportunities abroad or in the UK, but be certain that you have the patience and temperament for this work.

Contacts
The British Council Education and Training Group, 10 Spring Gardens, London SW1A 2BN
020 7930 8466   www.britishcouncil.org

Trinity College
www.trinitycollege.co.uk

Cambridge ESOL
www.cambridgeesol.org

Theatre Wardrobe Designer/Assistant (Costume Designer)

The job of theatre wardrobe designer can include anything from designing, creating, maintaining and repairing costumes to alterations and historical costume research. The work can be for theatre groups, TV, film and video companies, touring, national and regional theatre companies, or independent production companies. Costume designers have to have the technical knowledge to put a costume together, including accessories, as well as the creative eye and sense of historical accuracy to ensure the details are correct.

The Job Description
A typical day might include organisation of pre-set costume changes according to script demands. It may involve discussions with the director and set designers about the look of the production. It may require creative input on costumes for all actors, even walk-on parts. It may include arrangements for hire of costumes and fittings, or complete design of specific costumes. There may be alterations required for certain costumes or tailoring work to be undertaken.

The Person Specification
Costume designers may start as wardrobe assistants or costume supervisors, in which role they will be required to be multi-skilled in sewing, designing, fitting, altering and researching. They will deal with actors, arrange costume loans and visit costume exhibitions for ideas or research. The costume designer may be responsible for the visual look of a film or play and have to liaise with set designers, lighting production and staff to bring together the total visual presentation of the whole play or programme. You would need to be:

- interested in sewing, materials and textiles
- creative and fascinated by clothing design
- interested in history and knowledgeable about period detail
- good with people
- well organised
- passionate about visual arts and the theatre.

What It Takes
The three most common ways to train for this work are as follows: via a fashion design/textile design degree course; via a specialist theatrical costume design course; or through tailoring training. For entry to fashion/textile design courses, a foundation art course after A levels/Diploma or equivalent is often required, along with a good portfolio of examples

of design work. Theatrical costume courses are often available at drama schools (see Conference of Drama Schools for costume courses) or as specialist options at art schools. Normally, a good portfolio of design ideas, a foundation art course and A levels/Diploma or equivalent in art and history are recommended.

Tailoring training is still possible through apprenticeship schemes and through some City & Guilds courses at colleges.

Skillset recommends certain courses for those wishing to get into this work – check their website. For example, Angels Costumiers offers an 18-month New Entrant Wardrobe Training Course (www.angels.uk.com) and Film Skills Training offers a short course called 'Working in Wardrobe' (www.filmskills.org).

What Else
Work is generally on a freelance or short contract basis. Designers have to develop a reputation and use professional contacts to network themselves into further work.

What It Pays
This is difficult to gauge due to the range of employers, which may include a fringe theatre company, a regional theatre, a West End musical company, a film or TV company, or an opera company. Fees are based on a lump sum payment per production, including the time spent from pre-production, through rehearsals to the opening night or completion of filming; this may be three months' work on average, possibly shorter with some theatre productions or much longer with film productions.

Typically, film work pays best at around £10,000–£40,000 per production, theatres may pay between £600 and £3,000 per play, with West End musicals and opera companies paying between £3,500 and £10,000 for a run of a production. Some designers with small theatre companies may only be paid £200 per week. On average designers in theatre work may earn in the region of £12,000–£25,000 per year. Fee rates for these contracts are normally negotiated by an agent, so they can vary according to the experience and reputation of the designer. Certain directors may have a preference for certain designers, so being able to make a good impression on directors and producers is vital.

Prospects
This can be a highly competitive area of work, so establishing a working relationship with directors is necessary.

Best Advice
Develop a good portfolio of ideas and designs. Develop life-drawing/figure-drawing skills and carry a sketch book at all times. It is recommended that you develop a collection of sketches of different body

types that can be used in designs at a later stage. Immerse yourself in period detail before working on designs. Take short courses in sewing and tailoring techniques. Offer to work for free for amateur dramatic groups and volunteer for stage/set work at a local theatre.

Contacts

Skillset, 21 Caledonian Road, London N1 9GB
020 7713 9800   www.skillset.org

The Conference of Drama Schools
www.drama.ac.uk

Theatrical/TV Make-up Artist

The clue in the above title is the word 'artist' – this tells you that this job doesn't just involve applying make-up, but is more about using the best make-up and hairstyling techniques to create the most appropriate look for a model, TV presenter or theatrical/TV performer. Make-up artists have to interpret make-up requirements according to the play, film or programme that they are working on in order to satisfy their clients.

The Job Description

The make-up artist may work on a freelance, short contract or permanent basis for TV companies, theatres or for individual clients, and the work involves clarifying first of all what is required; then it may include research into a historical period, reading the script or sketching out possible ideas for the proposed 'look' required. Techniques might be corrective or involve the use of latex, character creation or elaborate special effects. Hairdressing is an essential part of the process, and basic hairdressing skills, as well as wigmaking and the use of hair pieces, are required.

The Person Specification

This career requires a mix of the practical and the creative. You will need to have good visualisation skills and an ability to translate ideas into reality. You will need to be:

- practical and artistic
- imaginative and have an ability to come up with ideas
- skilled at hairdressing and make-up techniques
- able to build rapport with clients through good verbal communication skills and focused listening
- good at networking and making contacts, as most make-up artists are self-employed.

What It Takes

There is no particular way to train for this career, but here are some ideas. There are combined hairdressing and beauty therapy courses at many colleges (normally NVQ or BTEC courses), which would give you a good grounding in the hairdressing and make-up skills needed. There are follow-on courses available in theatrical and media make-up which would also be useful. University degree courses in fine art, fashion, drama/ theatre studies, photography or film/media could also lead into this career. It is most important to develop practical skills and a portfolio of work, which may include photos or drawings. Many drama schools offer related courses – see the Conference for Drama Schools for courses.

Skillset lists a range of courses that are available, including some short courses through the London College of Fashion (www.fashion.arts.ac.uk) in film and TV make-up, and BTEC National Awards in make-up for TV and film, and special effects make-up.

What Else
Self-promotion and networking is vital as competition for work is intense. You may need to employ an agent in order to secure regular contracts. You may have to be prepared to re-locate for work and travel is a common feature of the job.

What It Pays
Salary details are difficult to gauge, due to the fact that the work is often freelance, but rates of pay start at around £15,000 per year; daily freelance rates may be from £100–£300 per day.

Prospects
Few permanent positions exist, so prospects depend on reputation, use of contacts and networking.

Best Advice
Make direct contact with professionals who do this work and ask to shadow them. Offer to work for free for an amateur dramatics group. Start building a portfolio of examples of your work. Gain any knowledge you can through research into period or historical make-up and be prepared to show you have an understanding of lighting techniques, colours, special effects and design.

Contacts
Skillset, 21 Caledonian Road, London N1 9GB
020 7713 9800   www.skillset.org

The Conference of Drama Schools
www.drama.ac.uk

TV/Film/Video Editor

There are several certainties about working in the film, TV or video industry: it will mean intense competition for work, possibly expensive training, and contract-to-contract or freelance work. Nonetheless, the idea of this kind of work can seem extremely appealing, so it's worth getting beyond the ideal to the reality to see if it would really suit you. TV, film and video editors are often considered to be the people who can save a bad film, make an actor look good or further enhance a good film. Many people in the industry would say that the film or programme is made in the cutting room, where the editor works with the raw footage, cutting and joining sequences and making sound and action synchronise (synching). This may still be done in the traditional manual way, but it has increasingly been replaced by digital technology, so digital cutting using specialist computer software may be the main way film is edited.

The Job Description

Film editors deal with film reels made up of camera shots, probably recorded onto video tape. The director will want to know whether the initial 'rushes' are technically good in case re-takes are going to be necessary. As re-takes can be expensive, the editor has to give advice as to whether this is necessary or whether the faults can be corrected digitally. Once this is decided, the editor will start to synch the film and soundtrack using specialist computer software. The film then needs to be sequenced according to the script and so the story takes shape. Discussions with the director as to sequences which need to be added or cut take place, and eventually the final cut will be ready.

TV/video editors are involved in a similar process, bringing together a programme or video according to the demands of the director, using video tape or digital recording equipment. Editing equipment is used to piece together the shots according to the script.

Sound editors use equipment to create and edit the soundtrack by selecting sound effects and music. Digital technology is used to record the sound onto disks so that it can be mixed and cut according to requirements. This work is, in effect, high-level sound engineering.

The Person Specification

There are some general requirements for all editing work. It often involves working long hours in an editing suite and you would need to be:

- quite a perfectionist
- able to work for long periods on your own

- able to concentrate for chunks of time and to pay attention to detail
- highly skilled with either excellent visual skills (film/TV/video editor) or excellent hearing (sound editor)
- competent at dealing with high-tech equipment
- interested in working with digital technology
- tactful when dealing with directors to tell them why you think the film needs to be cut.

What It Takes

Film/TV/video editors can train in a number of ways. Some will have started editing their own videos or have been involved in editing as part of a college media production course.

Sound editors might have taught themselves the basics of mixing and editing by doing DJ work.

Practical experience and learning through interest can be very useful, but most people who do this work have studied at college, and possibly university, on specialist courses.

It is worth checking out websites for the Broadcasting Entertainment Cinematographic and Theatre Union (BECTU) and Skillset for advice on accredited and recommended courses that would give you the skills you need. The National Film and Television School is world renowned and so there is intense competition for places, so you would need to show determination and evidence of your skills to gain a place on their editing or screen sound courses.

Make sure that any media, broadcast or film course you take has a substantial practical and skills component, preferably with work placements in the video/TV/film industry.

What Else

FT2 is a national provider of training for freelance careers in film and TV, and their funded training programmes are an excellent way of getting the skills and experience you need. They offer places on a training programme (once a year) to be an assistant editor through their new entrant technical training programme. Trainees are paid while they train and have work placements with film and TV companies so this scheme is very popular and only the best applicants get through. If you get through the application stage, you would be expected to show examples of your work, such as a VHS showreel, stills photographs or a sound recording at interview. Most applicants have developed these production/technical skills at a college or university.

Gaining confidence and competence in using specialist software such as Avid and Final Cut is paramount, and short course training for these skills is offered by private companies and advertised on the Skillset website.

What It Pays

This will be variable depending on whether the work is freelance or short-contract based, and on whether you are working for a small production company or on a big-name film. Skilled editors can often make a film a success in the cutting room (by brilliant editing and cutting) so pay also depends on skill and reputation.

Prospects

Editing work is often a good preparation for directing as the skills gained are so specialist.

Best Advice

Start in any way you can to practise editing with video, film or sound. Ask to work for free for a production company. Many people start off as a runner (see page 185), doing anything on a film set in order to make contacts and get the chance to learn the skills. Do a recommended course and get any work experience placement you can.

Contacts

Skillset, 21 Caledonian Road, London N1 9GB
020 7713 9800   www.skillset.org

Broadcasting, Entertainment, Cinematograph and Theatre Union (BECTU)
www.bectu.org.uk

National Film and Television School
www.nftsfilm-tv.ac.uk

FT2
www.ft2.org.uk

TV Presenter

This is one of those jobs that always seems appealing, but you need to be very sure that you have the talent, skills and motivation to pursue a career in television or the media. Working for television companies requires single-minded dedication and hard work if you are to achieve success in what is a most competitive industry.

The Job Description

You probably have some idea what presenters do, as part of their job can be seen on screen. They have to interview guests, provide links between programmes and read news items. They have to discuss issues and have a sense of what will interest the viewing public. What you might not realise is how much preparation is involved before you see the on-screen bit. This preparation involves discussing and devising programme ideas with a director or producer, researching items or guests and writing scripts for segments of news or interest items.

The Person Specification

The experience required will depend on the type of presenting being done. News presenters have to be extremely knowledgeable about current affairs, football commentators about football, music presenters about music, etc. But being knowledgeable is not enough, as communication skills to present information interestingly, to be able to think on your feet, to stay calm when necessary and to be comfortable on camera are also vital. You will need to be:

- confident and outgoing
- a quick learner with a good memory
- able to brief interviewees and make them feel welcome and calm
- interested in people and current events
- gifted at writing and speaking on camera in a natural way
- able to work well in a team.

What It Takes

There is no one way into this kind of work and no specific qualifications are laid down for entry to this career. In practice, presenters frequently have broadcasting or journalistic training and experience, either through Foundation degree or degree study for subjects like media or drama or journalism or even broadcast journalism/broadcasting studies. College courses prior to university in media studies offer students the chance to make their own videos, programmes and radio shows, and to develop the skill and confidence with media technology that is needed. Some people start in local radio, gaining experience, and then move into TV work.

What Else

Work experience on a newspaper, at a local radio station or with any public events or public speaking will be an advantage when applying for jobs. It is possible to apply for work experience at the BBC, but places are limited and competition is intense, so you will need to be keen and determined – check www.bbc.co.uk/workexperience for placements.

What It Pays

Pay rates depend on types of contract being worked; many TV staff work on a freelance or short-contract basis. Starting salaries can be in the range £15,000–£20,000 per year.

Prospects

Gaining a full-time job as a presenter will not be easy. Many people gain experience in hospital radio (www.hospitalradio.co.uk) or on a college newspaper and then forge a career path through journalism or radio, hoping for a break into TV. Experience, qualifications and commitment are needed to gain first jobs, then subsequent promotion.

Best Advice

Offer to work for free to gain experience. Research which university courses can offer you placements within TV companies. Be ready to apply for vacancies using a 'showreel' (a CD or DVD clip of about three–four minutes showing you talking to camera) of yourself presenting an item; this example of your presenting skills will allow potential employers to see and hear your broadcast voice and presence. Look out for competitions and trainee schemes offered by the BBC and Channel 4, such as the recent 'My Chance' trainee journalist scheme offered by the BBC.

Contacts

Skillset, 21 Caledonian Road, London N1 9GB
020 7713 9800   www.skillset.org

BBC
www.bbc.co.uk/talent or www.bbc.co.uk/workexperience

Channel 4
www.channel4.com/4careers

National Film and Television School
www.nftsfilm-tv.ac.uk

Underwriter

Insuring against risk is a crucial part of modern life, whether it is insurance to protect someone against cancellation of a holiday, medical expenses or in case the roof of a house is blown off. Although a call to an insurance company will normally result in a quote, this is not done in a casual way. Underwriters work for insurance companies and are responsible for assessing the risk factors associated with, for example, a holiday or driving a car, taking into account all possible eventualities. Once these factors have been assessed, the underwriter has to decide on the premium – or cost – for insurance. This could involve insuring a professional footballer against injury and loss of income or it could mean insuring a farm tractor against accidental damage.

The Job Description

Underwriters receive a proposal, or request, for insurance, which might be for personal, social or business reasons. They have to study the information provided and assess the likelihood of a future insurance claim on the basis of certain risk factors which can be possible or probable. A young driver with little experience may be presumed to be at greater risk of an accident than an experienced driver, and so the premium will be assessed at a higher rate. Certain insurance policies use standard procedures, such as computer software designed for insurance brokers to calculate risk and the price of a premium. However, for less usual situations, the underwriter may have to measure the risk, calculate the odds of a claim and issue an individual policy, quoting for special conditions or circumstances.

The Person Specification

Underwriters have to make sure that they have all the relevant information required to make a good decision, and this means that they have to ask intelligent questions and seek out background information. They have to be comfortable checking statistical information and be able to make decisions on whether to offer insurance cover or not. For this work, you would need to be:

- confident at taking responsibility for insurance decisions
- analytical and numerate when assessing statistical data
- good with computers, especially using databases and programs
- commercially minded, with an interest in insurance, taxation and the law
- good at problem solving
- able to communicate clearly in writing or verbally.

What It Takes
Most underwriters train on the job, taking Chartered Institute of Insurance (CII) exams by day release, evening study or distance learning. Entry to these courses is accepted for people with two A levels/Diploma or equivalent, or insurance qualifications such as the Certificate in Insurance Practice or the Financial Planning Certificate. Many companies offer underwriting traineeships to graduates of any degree or those with degrees in subjects like risk management, insurance or finance.

What Else
This work can carry the heavy responsibility of a costly mistake to an insurance company if an underwriter doesn't fully measure the risks of insurance.

What It Pays
Starting salaries are between £18,000 and £24,000 per year.

Prospects
Some underwriters specialise in particular types of insurance, while others with experience may supervise other underwriting staff. The more experienced an underwriter is, the more high-risk insurance they will assess.

Best Advice
Develop your computer skills and work hard at maths. Try to organise work experience in an insurance company to gain background knowledge of the industry. Contact the CII, which has a list of relevant degree courses for this work.

Contacts
The Chartered Insurance Institute, 42–48 High Road, South Woodford, London E18 2JP
020 8989 8464   www.cii.co.uk

Veterinary Nurse/Assistant

This may seem a dream job for someone who is passionate about animal care, but it requires a range of skills and experience, including some sound common sense. Remember that along with assisting the vet to care for animals, veterinary nurses also have to be involved in the decision to put an animal down and although this might be a highly sensible decision, it could be upsetting for an animal lover.

The Job Description
Veterinary nurses work mainly with domestic pets such as cats and dogs, but some may also work with larger animals like cows and horses. They assist the vet in the treatment and care of these animals, which can mean holding animals for examination, assisting during operations, giving anaesthetic and sterilising equipment, taking urine or blood specimens and generally monitoring an animal's condition. This job can be messy and even a little gory.

The Person Specification
A veterinary nurse can be based in a surgery or may travel out to appointments with the vet. They have to deal with emergencies and everyday treatments. They may advise on vaccinations, neutering and pet care, and they may have to give medication to an animal. They deal with drug ordering and run the reception desk, including taking telephone calls. They have to be skilled at dealing with animals and their owners. You would need to be:

- calm and capable under pressure
- patient with animals and their owners
- interested in the health and welfare of animals
- unafraid of animals in pain
- a good communicator, with an ability to deal with stressed owners.

What It Takes
To be accepted for the Royal College of Veterinary Surgeons (RCVS) veterinary nursing training scheme, you would need five GCSEs at C grade and over, or equivalent, including English and maths or a science, preferably both. You would need to be working at an approved RCVS training centre. Many nurses train on the job with a vet, as a trainee nurse while taking an RCVS veterinary nursing course on a day- or block-release basis at a local college. Following this, they may progress to the Diploma in Advanced Veterinary Nursing which is recommended for veterinary nurses as useful career progression by the RCVS.

There is a new role in surgeries called Animal Nurse Assistant (ANA) which requires lower GCSE qualifications and may be a starting role that could lead to further training. ANAs assist the veterinary nurse but may not be involved in operative procedures.

There are also new degree and Foundation degree courses on offer in subjects like veterinary nursing or veterinary nursing and practice management at various universities for those with A level/Diploma, or equivalent, qualifications.

Some colleges also offer introductory animal care courses at NVQ and BTEC level. These courses offer a good grounding in animal care, plus work placements which could be at a veterinary surgery. They could help you look a more convincing applicant when applying for a place as a trainee nurse.

What Else
Make sure that any course you take is accredited by the RCVS and research the work on the British Veterinary Nurse Association (BVNA) website as well.

What It Pays
Animal care jobs are frequently low paid, with staff happy to work because they love animals. Typical starting salaries for qualified nurses are in the range of £15,000–£24,000 per year.

Prospects
This is a small profession, with only about 5,000 qualified veterinary nurses employed in the UK. Jobs come up in veterinary practices, veterinary hospitals and with animal care charities such as the RSPCA and the PDSA. There is generally competition for jobs when they are advertised.

Best Advice
Voluntary work experience in RSPCA or PDSA animal care centres is valuable. Animal care college courses are a good introduction to this work. If you have your own pet, ask your own vet if you could do some workshadowing in the veterinary practice.

Contacts
Royal College of Veterinary Surgeons, Belgravia House, 62–64 Horseferry Road, London SW1P 2AF
020 7222 2001   www.rcvs.org.uk

The British Veterinary Nursing Association (BVNA)
www.bvna.org.uk

The People's Dispensary for Sick Animals (PDSA) is a charity that offers treatment to sick animals and runs 45 animal hospitals throughout Britain. They have a volunteer scheme that can be contacted by a freephone number (0800 854 194) or check their website: www.pdsa.org.uk

Viticulturalist

A viticulturalist may seem an unusual job title but in simple terms it means someone who is an expert in growing grapes for winemaking, a specialist branch of agriculture and horticulture which is focused on vineyards. While this might seem to you an unlikely UK-based job, there are, in fact, increasing work opportunities in the wine industry in the UK and abroad. Although the industry in the UK is small (about 400 vineyards), it nonetheless offers interesting work possibilities for someone who wants an outdoor and active job connected to the wine industry.

The Job Description

A viticulturalist will be responsible for a range of activities including grape variety selection, choice of site, establishment of optimum growing conditions, site maintenance and harvesting. Everything connected to the cultivation and success of a grapevine will be their responsibility. This means that they could be pruning vines or checking for pests, irrigating soil, applying fertilisers or actually picking the grapes. At certain times of the year hours of work will be long and the outdoor lifestyle might be the chief attraction of this work. Other less practical, more business-related activities might involve office-based planning work, checking yields and deciding on growing strategies. If the vineyard has a winery then it will also involve winemaking processes, tours and tastings.

The Person Specification

Viticulturalists are people who are interested in wine and growing processes. You would need to be:

- passionate about wine and the art of cultivating vines
- prepared to get your hands dirty and to work outdoors
- interested in the science of wine growing
- happy to work with machinery and pesticides.

What It Takes

Many people start by grape picking for a summer vacation to get a sense of what life on a vineyard is like. It is possible to enter the industry as a vineyard operative and learn on the job. You might take a horticultural course at college in the first place and then apply for jobs in vineyards – this might be the NVQ (or equivalent) in Land Based Operations at Level 1, followed by Production Horticulture at Level 2. If you want to progress beyond working as an operative on a vineyard you could take a Foundation degree in wine production, or the degree in Viticulture and Oenology at Plumpton College (University of Brighton). For Foundation degrees, GCSEs or equivalent, at C grade and over, in English, maths and science, and one A level/Diploma, or equivalent, will be required. For a degree, the same GCSE profile is needed, along with two–three A levels/ Diploma, or equivalent, preferably including a biological science. Some people even choose to study abroad in winemaking regions in New Zealand, Australia or California.

What Else
Learning about the finished product is a good idea, so check out the Wine and Spirits Education Trust (WSET) courses.

What It Pays
Starting salaries are around £15,000 per year for qualified staff.

Prospects
You could plan to have your own vineyard eventually, or develop particular expertise in research as a winemaking consultant.

Best Advice
Try some grapepicking work in France or further afield – you will get to know what the work involves and whether it would be right for you.

Contacts
Plumpton College, Ditchling Road, Lewes, East Sussex BN7 8AE (part of University of Brighton)
01273 890454   www.plumpton.ac.uk

Wine and Spirit Education Trust (WSET)
www.wset.co.uk

Webmaster/Website Designer

Webmasters and website designers are responsible for creating, designing and sometimes running a website for an organisation. The job titles are fairly interchangeable. The work involves finding out from the customer what is required, giving advice on possible formats and then designing and programming the website, including any possible graphics, video material or animation.

The Job Description

Web designers may create websites to promote an organisation or to provide information. They would discuss the content with the customer, advise on set-up and running costs, and then create the proposed site, taking into account customer feedback. A webmaster may also deal with the administration and maintenance of the site, updating it and resolving technical difficulties. If a site is used to take bookings or sell products or services, the webmaster will build in credit payment features so that orders can be taken and processed.

The Person Specification

Gifted webmasters and web designers are highly sought after. They have to have strong computer programming skills, with knowledge of specific packages like DreamWeaver or Flash. They will also be skilled in coding/scripting through programming languages such as HTML/XML and JavaScript. They have to be customer focused and creative. You would need to be:

- ready to keep yourself up to date with new developments and specialist packages
- multi-skilled in programming, graphics and multimedia
- able to understand an organisation's needs
- able to present website proposals in a persuasive manner
- able to train other staff in maintenance of the website.

What It Takes

Many web designers have degree/Foundation degree qualifications in multimedia design, digital media, computer graphics, computer science, information technology or software engineering, which all teach strong programming skills. Some people go into this job after teaching themselves DreamWeaver or web design packages, as employers sometimes recruit based on examples of outstanding work. If you can showcase 'live' websites which you have designed to an employer, then they may be persuaded by your talent alone. Keeping up to date with web design packages is crucial for this career.

What Else

This career requires a mixture of creative and technical skills. The programming side requires strong numerical skills, and most programming/software engineering degree courses require maths at A level standard.

More creative courses may accept applicants with design skills who are comfortable using technology.

What It Pays

Gifted webmasters may be able to name their price, but typical starting salaries are in the range of £15,000–£20,000 per year.

Prospects

There is an incredible growth in multimedia opportunities, so job prospects are good.

Best Advice

Work hard at maths and develop creativity. Teach yourself web design and create your own CV website which showcases your own work – employers might find you by trawling the net and decide to headhunt you.

Contacts

British Computer Society, First Floor, Block D, North Star House, North Star Avenue, Swindon, Wiltshire SN2 1FA
01793 417417   www.bcs.org

British Interactive Multimedia Association
www.bima.co.uk

UK Web Design Association
www.ukwda.org

Wedding Planner

Although this job might sound well suited to an incurable romantic, the reality is that wedding planners have to be organised, professional and businesslike in the way they support couples in planning the perfect wedding or civil partnership. Planners take all the responsibility for arranging the event, sourcing flowers, entertainment, catering, and even finding a venue if necessary. They plan everything in the finest detail so that their customers can really enjoy the occasion.

The Job Description

The wedding planner will start by meeting the couple, and possibly other family members, and will find out what ideas the bride and groom or partners have. The planner will talk through the key aspects to be considered such as the place for the ceremony, venue for the reception, transport, decorations, music, entertainment and photography. They will map out what is required, discuss budgets and make recommendations. They advise on etiquette, place settings, themed weddings, civil partnership laws and can deal with last-minute problems and high emotions. As weddings can be costly, the planner's ability to manage the process and keep it all within budget is of paramount importance.

The Person Specification

Planners need to be multi-skilled and business-minded. They have to have an eye for detail and a practical, common-sense approach. For this job you would need to be:

- a good listener
- able to interact well with all kinds of people
- willing to learn about the hospitality industry
- a good networker – someone who makes useful contacts and keeps a track of different services that might be available
- financially confident – able to plan and run a business and keep account of money spent
- creative and a problem solver.

What It Takes

Most wedding planners working today have trained in the hotel/hospitality industry, probably through on-the-job training with NVQs or equivalent in hospitality and catering, or through university courses in hospitality or event management. GCSEs or equivalent (at D grade and above) will allow you to do an apprenticeship or college course in hospitality. For degree courses A level/Diploma qualifications and a good GCSE profile including English and maths at C grade and over, or equivalent, will be needed.

There are some short courses specific to wedding planning such as the one offered by the UK Alliance of Wedding Planners (UKAWP) (one or two day courses) or the Diploma in Wedding Planning through the Institute of Wedding Planners (nine months through distance learning), which may offer a useful introduction to this work.

What Else
Working hours can be unsocial, including long days and evening meetings with customers.

What It Pays
Starting salaries for wedding planners are in the region of £16,000–£20,000 but freelance planners normally ask for a fee which is 20 per cent of the cost of the wedding – this might mean paying a fee of £2,000–£3,000 or more.

Prospects
Many planners start off working for major hotel groups and once experienced, move into freelance work. The complexity of planning a wedding event means that planners can progress into other areas of conference or event management very easily.

Best Advice
Start collecting information about wedding event suppliers. Visit wedding fairs run by major hotels. Work hard at business subjects and try and gain experience with a wedding planner or hotel event organiser.

Contacts
People 1st, 2nd Floor, Armstrong House, 38 Market Square, Uxbridge, Middlesex UB8 1LH
0870 060 2550   www.people1st.co.uk

The UK Alliance of Wedding Planners
www.ukawp.com

Institute of Professional Wedding Planners
www.inst.org/wedding-planner-courses

X-Ray Assistant/ Radiography Assistant

Radiography assistants work alongside qualified diagnostic and therapeutic radiographers, supporting and assisting them in their work. On the diagnostic side, radiography is about using ionising radiation and imaging techniques such as ultrasound to diagnose various diseases or illnesses or to check and monitor someone's progress. On the therapeutic side, radiography is used to treat diseases such as cancer through the use of radiation.

The Job Description

Being an assistant in a radiology department is not just about administering X-rays to check for injuries; it can involve using various imaging technologies including ultrasound, magnetic resonance imaging and nuclear medicine. You might be supporting the radiographer on the diagnostic side, setting up equipment and ensuring the safe use of radiation and providing a service for many different hospital departments – such as the accident and emergency department, outpatients or the operating theatres and wards. On the therapeutic side, you may be supporting patients throughout their cancer treatment and working with a team of medical professionals in charge of a patient's care.

The Person Specification

Many patients become anxious in a hospital, and presenting them with high-tech equipment, which may seem threatening, can make the situation very stressful. A radiography assistant needs to have good people skills to reassure patients about the procedures that they may have to undergo. You would need to be:

- a good communicator
- sensitive and calm
- confident in dealing with high-tech equipment
- able to learn new techniques in a fast-moving occupation
- interested in health and with a knowledge of anatomy
- prepared to be careful and pay attention to detail, especially when dealing with radiation.

What It Takes

Most radiography assistant posts ask for a good general education, preferably with four GCSEs, probably at C grade and above, or equivalent, including English and a science. Training is on the job and a caring and empathic temperament is valued, especially for the therapeutic radiography areas. Sometimes there are trainee assistant practitioner posts within radiographic areas in the NHS. These can lead into this career and allow further training for a Foundation degree in primary care or health care. For trainee assistant practitioner posts an A level/Diploma qualification or NVQ Level 3 in care is required.

What Else
Most assistants are employed by the NHS in hospitals, but there are jobs in clinics and private sector health organisations. There is much more work on the diagnostic side than on the therapeutic side.

What It Pays
Typical starting salaries for radiography assistants are in the range £14,000–£17,257 per year, with assistant practitioners earning £14,000–£20,000 per year.

Prospects
Many people try out the job as an assistant, later going on to train for radiography; at least two A levels/Diploma or equivalent, including one science, and a range of GCSEs at C grade and over, or equivalent, would be required for full radiography degree-level training which takes three years. It helps to have a knowledge of human biology and physics for radiography work.

Best Advice
Contact your local hospital radiography department, as it may be possible to work-shadow or act as a volunteer to an assistant to check out this job.

Contacts
Society of Radiographers, 207 Providence Square, Mill Street, London SE1 2EW
020 7740 7200   www.sor.org

NHS Careers
www.nhscareers.nhs.uk

Zookeeper

It's fairly obvious that the main responsibility of a zookeeper is to care for the variety of animals that a zoo contains, but these days all zoo staff are involved in a wider range of roles. These might include marketing, retailing and general visitor management. Nonetheless, the animal management part of a zookeeper's job involves the caring for, and nurturing of, a variety of animals, including feeding and watering, and checking for injury and ill-health. Being close to the animals on a day-to-day basis means that zookeepers are the best people to notice a small change in an animal's behaviour or health. They are also increasingly involved in the protection of certain dwindling species through planned breeding programmes and educational activities.

The Job Description
Daily routines involve mucking out and cleaning pens and cages, preparation of food – including vitamin supplements – and providing clean water and bedding. It may involve hand rearing a marmoset or a giraffe, or dealing with big cats. Zookeepers have to make detailed observations of animals for signs of illness or injury, ensure the safety of animals and visitors, and keep paths and garden areas clean and tidy. As a zookeeper, you would also be required to handle visitor enquiries, get involved in special events and even give short talks.

The Person Specification
An enthusiasm and interest for animals and a commitment to increasing the quality of their life is vital. You would need to be knowledgeable about the animals' habits and natural habitats and be able to communicate this knowledge to visitors. You would need:

- good communication skills
- an ability to do hard, physical work
- to be patient with animals and the visitors
- to be responsible about safety.

What It Takes
Although no specific qualifications are required, a good education including biological subjects is useful, and a strong interest in animals and conservation is valuable. There are some excellent animal care or management courses at many colleges across the country. These include NVQ or BTEC courses and the City & Guilds course in Animal Management, devised in conjunction with the Association of British and Irish Wild Animal Keepers (ABWAK), provided through the National Extension College and recommended for trainee keepers.

Some people might decide to study for degrees in animal sciences or zoology, for which A levels/Diploma in biology and GCSEs at C grade and over (or equivalent) in maths, English and science will be expected. Typical degree courses are titled Wildlife Conservation with Zoo Biology; Salford University's course has an optional two-week placement in Tanzania, as well as a placement year for researching wildlife habitats in the UK or even in the Serengeti.

What Else

There is intense competition for jobs, with only about 1,500 people working in zoos and wildlife parks in Britain, so there are always many more applicants than actual job vacancies. If you can arrange some work experience in a zoo or with animals, this would be a useful first step. There may be seasonal jobs with some zoos or wildlife parks, which would be a good way into permanent jobs at a later stage. Some zoos may operate a volunteer scheme, which would be an ideal way to experience the work of a zoo first hand. Most people in zoos work for love of animals and the animals in danger of extinction.

What It Pays

Starting salaries can be around £14,000 per year, with experienced zookeepers earning between £15,000 and £20,000 per year.

Prospects

There are chances of promotion to senior keeper and then head keeper, but they can be limited due to the availability of suitable jobs. Some keepers move into other areas of animal care and have to move to other zoos for promotion.

Best Advice

Associate membership of ABWAK is recommended as a way of staying well informed about the work of zoos, including job vacancies. Details can be found on their website, along with lists of zoos in the UK.

Contacts

Association of British and Irish Wild Animal Keepers, c/o Edinburgh Zoo, 134 Corstorphine Road, Edinburgh EH12 6TS
0131 334 9171   www.abwak.co.uk

National Extension College, Michael Young Centre, Purbeck Road, Cambridge CB2 2HM
01223 400200   www.nec.ac.uk